Think Like a
GUY

To my beautiful mother,

Anna DePandi,

the strongest, most loving, and funniest person I
have ever met. You are simply incredible. Thank
you for making me the woman I am today. I would
be nothing without you.

Love,
Giuliana

Warning

No bullshit was used in the making of this book. It is honest, sometimes harsh, and can be unpleasant to read. Most important, it's straightforward and to the point. You won't find any annoying attempts at being clever instead of being simple. The point of this book isn't to try to impress you with metaphors and words you only find on the SATs.

Also, no thesaurus was used in the making of this book. If you are in search of over-descriptive sentences and four-syllable words, look elsewhere. This book was written as straight-up as possible. (As a matter of fact, I think "straight-up" isn't even in the thesaurus.) I'm writing this book to share some insight, not impress you with my amazing use of metaphors, similes, and hyperbole. Yes, "hyperbole" is a word.

Contents

Preface

Not long ago, I fell in love with the perfect guy: young, handsome, six-foot-three, successful, hysterically funny, caring, and loyal. I knew he was special the moment I met him. The morning of our first date, I was tipped off that this guy had a reputation for being a "player." Not because he was a bad boy at heart, but because he felt he'd never met a girl special enough to get him to settle down. I quickly realized I wanted to be that girl, the one he would fall for, the first girl he would truly love.

But in order for him to see me as the one, I was going to have to do things differently than everything he was used to, different from every girl before me. In fact, a male friend of mine said to me, "If hundreds of beautiful women can't land this guy, then how are you gonna land him?" I thought about it. Then I thought about it some more. I realized that the only way to beat out every other woman before me was to not make the mistakes all those other women had made. You know, those fatal mistakes that most girls make in the initial stages of dating?

So what did I do? I did the complete opposite of what all the girls before me did because in order to land the guy I wanted, I couldn't think like a girl. I had to think . . . like a guy.

Think Like a
GUY

Introduction

For centuries, when it came to getting a guy, women made the same mistakes over and over again. In modern times especially, most girls fall flat on their face before they ever make it to the altar. And no matter how many female-empowerment books or women's magazines we read, most of us just can't seem to get the man of our dreams to say those magic words, "Will you marry me?" Until now . . .

You see, I've learned that you can't land a man by reading all those female-empowerment books or women's magazines. In fact, you have to avoid those altogether. The way to land a guy is to think, act, and react . . . like a guy.

Have you ever seen a man get all goo-goo gaga over a baby in a grocery store line? *No!*

Have you ever seen a guy stop in his tracks at the sight of a cute puppy and start drooling over it? *Never!*

Have you ever gone out with a guy who on the first date starts telling you all about his fears and insecurities? *No way!*

Have you ever been three dates into a relationship and had a guy tell you his real desire in life is to quit his job and be a stay-at-home dad? *Absolutely not!*

Guys never commit any of these fatal mistakes, but women do. When men see babies, they look the other way. It takes a guy at least a few months to reveal his fears and insecurities. And no girl wants to hear a guy say he doesn't want a career and his only goal in life is to get married and have kids. That's simply unheard of. Women need a guide that points out exactly what they are doing wrong and exactly what men are doing right.

Men are not complex creatures. We think they're complex because we can never seem to figure them out. But in reality, they're pretty simple to break down once you realize they don't think like women think. Even if you meet a guy and you're convinced he's the exception—convinced he thinks like you do and not like other guys—you're wrong. At the end of the day, guys look at something one way, and girls look at the same thing another way. Plain and simple.

Therefore, in order to get the guy you really want, you can't make the same mistakes all the women before you made. You know, the women who couldn't land him. The women who couldn't get him to commit. The women he passed up. No, my friend, you cannot go down the same path these women went down. In fact, you have to get off that path completely. You have to possess the tips that men subconsciously live by, the tips this book will reveal to you. Because in the end, the best way to land a guy is by thinking like one.

It's simple. This book will train you to think . . . like a guy. Because dating has always been a guy's world, until now.

The Theory

Guys are naturally evasive, and they are attracted to evasive girls. Yes, evasive . . .

e•va•sive adj.

1. Deliberately vague or ambiguous
2. Avoiding or escaping from difficulty or danger, especially enemy fire
3. Skillful at eluding capture

*W*hy evasive, you ask? Men are hunters by nature. And it's not the capture, it's the hunt that really gets 'em going. There is nothing more unfulfilling to a man than easy prey. If a deer hunter lands his prey within the first five minutes he's in the woods, he'll experience an immediate sense of excitement. A big "Woo-Hoo." But listen to me when I tell you that the joy will wear off as quickly as it came, and in no time, he'll move on to his next victim.

Therefore, you have to let a guy sweat it out. Imagine this: A hunter enters the woods and after about seven or eight minutes, he spots his prey. He cocks his gun, takes aim, fires—and misses. No big deal. He cocks his gun again, takes aim, shoots—and misses again, and again, and again. After several attempts, he starts getting really frustrated. Does that mean he's gonna pack up and go home? Hell, no! In fact, he's gonna go after that one particular deer, the one that's a little too sly and won't take the bait. The one who . . . "evades" him.

Now the hunter is going after this one deer (who suddenly appears more strikingly beautiful than before) with a vengeance. After about eight more misses, he starts going nuts! He's gonna do whatever it takes to get his hands on that girl—oops! I mean doe. He's pulling out all the stops. Hours pass, daytime becomes dusk and he's never worked harder in his life to shoot a deer. After five hours and dozens of failed attempts, the hunter's vengeance turns to sadness. He hasn't seen the doe in close to an hour. As he sits against a tree, nearly defeated, he hears a rustle. He looks up, and there she is! His heart starts pounding, his brow gets sweaty. He says a prayer, takes a deep breath, and fires his forty-ninth bullet. And with that shot he strikes his prey right in the heart. He takes a moment to let it all sink in and drops to his knees in absolute glee. He's in total disbelief. He jumps to his feet and runs as fast as his legs will go and crouches right next to the defeated deer. Now, normally, the hunter drags his prey off to the side and goes on hunting. But unlike the dozens of other deer he's shot in the past, he treats this particular one with dignity. Instead of flinging it onto his flatbed truck, he delicately lifts it up and carefully lays it to rest in the back. He drives home extra slowly that night, and once he gets home, he cooks up and bites into the most delicious deer meat he's ever tasted. When he's through with the meal, do you suppose he throws the remains away? Oh no, this one's special, remember! Instead, he mounts the deer's head on the wall directly within eyeshot of his desk so he can admire it for years to come. He treasures that moment in the woods for the rest of his life every time he glances at that face. The one that almost got away.

Now let's get out of the woods and into the real world. If you play hard to get—very hard to get—then once you make him your boyfriend, he will treasure you like no other woman before you. Sounds simple, right? Well, not exactly—at least not for most girls. Women are generally more emotional than men; we experience feelings of love, bonding, and nurturing more intensely than a guy does. Obviously, this isn't true in every new relationship, but it is the case in the majority of them. We are just wired differently than our male counterparts. And the problem with us is that we accept that we are built a certain way, and too often we allow our emotions to get in the way of acting cool. Just check out the shelf at your local Blockbuster.

Movies geared toward women? Romantic comedies. Everything from *Pretty Woman* to *Bridget Jones's Diary*. Stories of women looking for love and lots of tears along the way.

Movies geared toward men? Action. Everything from *Rambo* to *The Fast and the Furious*. Basically, films with lots of banging and little effort required.

So the trick is to curb the behavior that oftentimes leads us to misery and tears. You know, falling for a guy after two dates and letting him know it, which leads to chasing him away with your intensity. You've gotta break this cycle, and I'm gonna help you break it by letting you in on the way guys look at things and handle situations. If I lay them all out for you and show you how to adapt them to your own life, then I strongly believe (from tons of experience) that you will have a better chance of landing the guy you are dying to land.

Back to the word "trick" for a minute. Some people may look at this book and think it's about tricking men into thinking we are something we aren't. But the fact is, women by nature are more selfless than men. We have been coined as nurturers since the beginning of time. The problem is, we now live in a new day and age. An age where it's becoming more and more acceptable to stay single longer. Guys used to get married at twenty-two and twenty-five years old. These days, some guys are waiting until their forties to take their first walk down the aisle. Why? Because they can. Because the guy you really like is making his own money and bought his own car and house. He really doesn't need anyone to lean on financially, and quite frankly, he is getting set in his own ways and likes his freedom. So for a girl to get him to settle down, she's gotta be really special. He'll want a girl that complements his life, not one who makes it worse by acting needy and pushy. Guys just won't tolerate that as much as they used to. And guys are becoming better at weeding out the needy girls from the cool girls. This means you need to appear less annoying and less high-maintenance than the girls he's dated in the past. You need to be more independent and confident, like most guys are. How do you do this? By caring more about yourself and less about making sure the man in your life is having his every whim catered to. Trust me, he will appreciate and respect you more without even realizing it.

We often accuse men of being too distracted, not caring enough about us. Just because they don't obsess over our every move doesn't mean they don't care about us. It's just that they care more about themselves. Period. And we need to start doing the same.

Here Are Some Essentials
Think Like a Guy Will Teach Girls

- Don't seem too interested in kids, babies, and puppies when they are around. Simply acknowledge them and move on. Don't get all mushy over them—he'll assume that you're dying to have a baby.
- When you first start dating, don't call him unless you have something to say. "I was just calling to say, 'What's up,' " is not something to say. When men make calls, they

have an objective, a reason they are calling. They can't tolerate sitting on the phone for hours at a time talking about nothing. But women can. Cut this behavior out.

▪ Never give away too much unnecessary information too early in the relationship. "I just found out I'm being audited by the IRS." Don't tell him, dummy! He'll figure he can't ever marry you because your stupidity and shady behavior will get him thrown in jail. And don't admit that your credit cards are maxed out or your credit rating is horrid. Men never admit these things early in the relationship, and those who do look like total losers in our eyes. Avoid looking like a loser.

▪ Don't reveal all your deepest, darkest secrets (a past eating disorder, childhood issues) until there is a ring on your finger. Many women confide too much in a man too early in the relationship, and it drives men away. Make a guy fall in love with you before you tell him that you were molested as a child or you were bulimic in college. Trust me, when it comes to the dark secrets, revealing less in the beginning is more.

▪ The first time you sleep over, wake up early and sneak out without saying good-bye or leaving a note. Don't be the girl who is smothering him when he wakes up, asking him to take you to brunch. You gotta admit, the guys who bail the next morning are the hottest, the ones who make us crazy! The ones who have us sitting by the phone, dying for them to call. Trust me, men react the same to a woman who bails without looking back. Yes, I'm sure. You obviously don't know because you've never tried it. Most women haven't—that's the problem.

▪ Don't be a finicky eater. If you have quirky eating habits, do not reveal them until he is officially your boyfriend.

▪ If you have a "dysfunctional" relationship with your parents or siblings or both, hide this from your man until well into the relationship.

▪ Don't keep asking him what he thinks of you and the relationship. "Do you love me?" "Do you think I'm pretty?" "What do you want out of this relationship?"

▪ Don't be the first to mention marriage or kids. Let him initiate this conversation. If a man really digs you from the start, he'll play around with the idea of marriage. When he does this, don't play along! Instead, seem relatively disinterested. It will make him crazy and he'll buy that ring now, not several years down the road. If you seem enthusiastic about marrying him too soon, you will turn him off and drive him away. It's simple: They always want what they can't have (or what is very hard to get).

▪ Don't discuss your past sex life. Never reveal how many guys you've really slept with. If it's over five, lie. They can't handle over five.

▪ Don't admit that you fall in love easily or that you've been in love *sooooo* many times. Actually, say you've never been in love. Guys wanna be the first. Except when it comes to sex. Past the age of twenty-one, guys are not interested in taking your virginity—it's too much emotional work and too messy, quite frankly. They want a girl not with experience, but with a natural ability—a girl just born sexy. And remember, it's sexy, not slutty. "Even though I've had so little experience, I just know what's up in the bedroom, ya know. I really believe you're either born with sex appeal or you're not. I feel so bad for those friends of mine that aren't. It must be tough." Try that line for starters—it's golden!

- When the phone conversation starts lagging on either end, no matter how bad you wanna lie in bed and chat with him about nothing, hang up the phone! Be the first to end the conversation. He'll be so shocked and intrigued that you had the balls to get off the phone first that he will make plans with you before you hang up.

- Don't cry while watching a sad movie until at least two months into the relationship. If you have the urge to cry, make a run for the bathroom or kitchen. If he catches you tearing up, say you yawned and are tearing naturally. Any sign of crying or tears can freak a guy out too early in the relationship.

- Don't doodle his name. Don't tell him his last name sounds good with your first name.

- Forget stuff (dates, anniversary, etc.) and blame it on your crazy schedule—he is not your priority.

- Don't bring up your best friend's new and great relationship. Instead, bring it up and say it's pathetic and lame.

- Never kiss on the first date, no matter how great it was or how much you are dying to kiss him.

- When you have your period or a medical condition that will keep you from fooling around, use that night to blow him off. Tell him you have plans on the nights that you are "out of commission." It's a great opportunity to seem aloof, without telling him why you are really skipping out on seeing him. It'll keep him on his toes.

- When he calls the first time, answer the phone with a touch of frenzy in your voice. I don't care if you are sitting in your car, twirling your hair in traffic. Sound busy. Don't tell him you are sitting in your car, twirling your hair in traffic. Say you are running late to a meeting or you are just leaving a meeting on your way to another appointment.

- Don't admit you were a lousy student in high school or college. If you were anything less than a B student, say you were a B student. Men don't like dumb girls, even if you were just lazy in high school. Never admit you got anything less than 1050 on your SATs. Adjust the score depending on how intelligent the guy is. He will never try to uncover your GPA or SAT score. Tell him you have no clue where the paperwork is. (I mean, who really holds on to old SAT results or report cards?)
- Always look put together and well-groomed. Women have a tendency to let themselves go once they have been in a relationship for a substantial amount of time. This is partly because the man makes us feel comfortable enough to be relaxed and throw on sweats and sneakers all the time, and even encourages us to dress down. The problem is, the next time you're at the movies in your sweats and sneakers with your man and some hot girl stands in front of you in the snack line and she's on a first date wearing sexy jeans and high heels, your man can't help but compare you to the girl. Guess who comes out on top? She does.

The Tips

Love 'em or hate 'em.
Agree with most and
disagree with others.
Embrace the ones you want
and dismiss the ones you
don't like.
But read them at your
own risk.
The risk of getting the
guy you really, really want.

TIP #1

Give Him Your Digits, But Don't Take His

If he digs you, he will call.

You meet a guy, he wants to exchange numbers. Hesitate for a minute. Hesitate for a minute more. Finally, give him your digits. He glances at your number and smiles, then gives you a look like it's his turn to give you his phone number. Whatever you do, don't ask for his phone number. When he offers to give it to you, decline it. If he insists, shrug your shoulders, cock your head slightly to the side, and say, "No, thanks. It's cool. You've got my number. I'm sure I'll talk to you soon." Why shouldn't you take his phone number? Here's the deal.

If a guy likes you and he wants to hang out with you and you give him your phone number, *he will call!* If he didn't really like you and has no intention of hanging out with you but he took your phone number anyway, *he won't call!* Make sense? If not, let me break it down into a basic equation. If algebra wasn't your thing, no biggie. I'll use simple arithmetic:

BOY GETS GIRL'S DIGITS + BOY LIKES GIRL = BOY CALLS GIRL

BOY GETS GIRL'S DIGITS + BOY DOESN'T LIKE GIRL
  = BOY DOESN'T CALL GIRL

Got it? Good! A+ for you. What you've done is left the ball in his court. Doesn't feel so good, does it? I assure you, if things go well, it may be the only time he ever has full control in your relationship.

Now that the fate of the first phone call rests on his shoulders, then what good is it having his phone number? In fact, having his number could actually be very damaging. If you have his number you will be tempted to call him. Especially after day 3 of not hearing a peep from Mr. I Totally Felt a Connection. And just think of how embarrassed you'll be when you call him four days after meeting him and he doesn't remember who you are out of the five girls he gave his number to that night. I know you may be saying, "Oh, but if I get his number instead of giving mine out, then the ball's in my court!" Listen, Kournikova, you gotta get on that tennis court before you can even get the ball.

Focus less on your backhand, and more on your need to avoid the embarrassment of a phone call that may lead to rejection. Instead, let him make the first move. I promise you, if he was hot for you that first night, *he will call!*

Jordan, age twenty-six, San Diego

I recently had an experience that made me think twice about giving my number to a girl ever again. I had gotten out of a serious relationship and was single for about three weeks when a college friend tried to set me up with a friend of hers (let's call her Julie) over a group dinner. So, at this group dinner I was relieved that Julie and I got along really well. We talked for most of the night and she seemed like a great girl, but I'd only been single a few weeks and couldn't just hop into another relationship. At the end of the night we exchanged numbers and I told her that I'd call her.

Now, I don't really believe in the three-day rule—it's crap. If you like someone, call them—it's not rocket science. Sometimes, however, shit happens and you can't call. We've all had weeks when it feels like the entire world is out to get you. Well, I was having one of those weeks. I was working long hours, fighting sickness, and dealing with getting my stuff back from my ex. It was the kind of week where I actually thought about giving up everything and moving to West Virginia to live in a trailer. I kept the I-need-to-call-this-girl thought at the back of my mind but I had a laundry list of shit to deal with before I got to her.

On the night of the fourth day that I didn't call Julie, my phone rings at about 12:15 A.M. I don't recognize the number, but I pick it up anyway (yeah, she called from a friend's phone—classy move, by the way). All of a sudden I'm getting bitched out by a voice I don't recognize, partly from the drunken slurring of her words but mostly because I'd only talked to this girl once in my entire life (oh yeah, and she sucker-punched me by calling from someone else's phone). This is a transcript of the first five seconds of the phone call:

ME: Hello?
HER: What kind of guy takes a girl's phone number and
doesn't call her, you asshole?!
ME: Uh . . .

She said way more, but that was the most coherent part of the new-asshole-ripping I received. After I realized who it was on the other end, I tried sincerely to apologize and explain myself. However, it was apparent that she had worked herself into a seething frenzy over me not calling and needed to vent, and by vent I mean verbally kick me in the groin.

I felt bad that she was so angry. To be honest, I probably could have called her the next day and straightened everything out; we might've even still been together, but after that little episode . . . why would I want to? ▪

TIP #2

The First Phone Call

■

Ring . . . Ring . . . Ring . . . Oh my gosh, it's him!

When he calls the first time, answer the phone with a touch of frenzy in your voice. I don't care if you are sitting in your car, twirling your hair in traffic. Sound busy. Don't tell him you are sitting in your car, twirling your hair in traffic. Say you are running late to a meeting or you are just leaving a meeting on your way to another appointment. Be vague. When he asks for details, say, "Oh, I'm just in the middle of some work stuff, no biggie. How ya doin'?" Immediately turn the conversation away from yourself and direct it back to him or something interesting that is happening in the news. "I was just listening to CNN on my XM radio and heard the verdict come down in the killing of that teenage girl in Florida. Have you heard it yet? No? Well, the jury found the defendant . . ." Nice. What a great first impression, huh? He'll think you're intelligent and worldly right off the bat. And, if you can't come up with anything interesting in the news, then simply direct the conversation his way and let him talk about himself. The reason? If you start talking about yourself too much, it could end in disaster. Most girls will just go into their whole life story in the very first phone call, and that is such a big no-no, it's not even funny. On the no-no scale of 1 to 10, it's a 9. Why? Because you must remain mysterious and evasive. Remember the definition of evasive? Let me refresh your memory.

e•va•sive adj.

1. Deliberately vague or ambiguous
2. Avoiding or escaping from difficulty or danger, especially enemy fire
3. Skillful at eluding capture

First and foremost, you need to save the relationship—and your peak-time minutes—by keeping your phone conversations brief and appearing "evasive" from the get-go. Let's practice.

You're sitting in traffic rocking out to your favorite song when your phone rings. So, gripped by the song, you answer without looking at your caller ID. *"My milkshake brings all the boys to the*—Oh, hello!?" "Hi, it's Troy. We met at the club on Friday night." Oh shit! It's Troy. Hot Troy. Trust-fund Troy. The first worthwhile guy you've met in a very, very long time. Caught off guard, you do your best to make the conversation work. You say hi, make some small talk, and then things get quiet. And awkward. And when he asks where you're driving, you blurt out the truth. "I'm headed to my therapist." Silence. More awkward small talk, and then Troy says he has to grab the other line and that he'll call you right back. Eight months pass without so much as a text message from Troy. What an inconsiderate jerk! Not that you're bitter, because you'd never date a guy shorter than you anyway, so of course you're not waiting by the phone. And what kind of name is Troy, anyway? Asshole.

Next time, avoid making the same mistake by keeping your conversations brief. In doing so, you will avoid the awkward pauses that lead to certain doom, either because he'll think you're boring and have nothing to say or because you'll feel obligated to end the silence and blurt out something absurdly stupid. You also run the risk of babbling when you stay on the phone too long, unarmed with good conversation points. Babbling too soon in the relationship—especially in the first phone call—can lead to sudden death. Even a simple "How ya doing today?" can lead to disaster. Keep your answers positive, short, and simple. In addition, don't go into a story that may turn him off completely. For example, never have certain conversations too early on. By "certain" I mean topics that should only be reserved for your best friend, mother, or sister. People who have known you for a at least a few years, not a few minutes.

GUY: Hey, Liz? It's Troy from last night. How's it going?

YOU: Oh, hey! Um, everything's good, thanks. Except I'm kinda freaking out because I'm stuck in traffic and I have the worst stomachache ever!

GUY: Man, I'm sorry to hear that. What happened?

YOU: It's a *loooong* story. But since you asked, I was at lunch with my friend and I ordered the tuna salad because that's what I always order when I go to Veneto Café. So the tuna comes and I'm eating it and it's all good and all of a sudden after ten minutes my stomach starts totally growling. [*Insert four more minutes of boring dialogue here.*] Then I'm like, running to the bathroom for the third time and I'm thinking "Ughh, this is so gross! What is wrong with me?" [*Insert three more minutes of excruciatingly boring dialogue.*] Because about a month ago I had a similar thing happen, which kept me in the bathroom for what seemed like days. But that wasn't because of tuna, that was after I ate some creepy bagel and lox at that restaurant on Third Street, the place with the amazing—

GUY [*makes fake cell phone static noise*]: Oh, wait, sorry Liz . . . think my phone . . . cutting out—call—later— bye.

So basically, disaster can happen in various shapes and sizes. It can come in the form of one simple three-second statement about the state of your mental health. It can also come in the form of an ten-minute short story of how you got a bad case of the runs. There really is no guideline on exactly how long conversations should last, as long as they are conducted properly.

Be sure, though, to always be the one to end the first few calls. Wrap up the conversation the second you feel it start to lag. Don't wait for him to say, "OK, well it was nice talking to you. I gotta go," simply because the two of you have run out of things to say. If that happens, he will be getting off the phone on a low note. God forbid, he may think you're boring! Instead, you must make the first move to get off the phone, especially if you are just a few minutes into the conversation and can't think of anything clever to talk about. Out of nowhere say, "Oh, wait! I just remembered something! I'll call you right back. What's your number?" (Yes, this is where you can get his number.) Once you hang up, think of three or four interesting things to talk about. If you can't think of anything, call a friend to get some news or ideas. Jot down some talking points and topics that will make you look smart or witty. Those don't include talking about the weather—or your ex.

OK, after you've made a little list, wait at least one hour to call him back. To be honest, I like to wait at least a few hours, sometimes an entire day. My best advice is not to call until the next day because it'll make you look busy and cool, not lonely and desperate. Especially after telling the guy you would call him "right back." That way he will be expecting your call from the second you hang up, and he'll be waiting all day. Brilliant! Remember, men don't like girls who come easy.

Note: With that said, I realize that this is only the second tip and you are probably not totally comfortable with this new way of thinking yet. So I'll cut you some slack and let you get by with calling him back after only one hour. I realize it's practically impossible for some women to wait an entire twenty-four hours to call back a new guy. I've given some of my best friends that advice and most don't listen. But the ones that do? Boy, do they hook their guy quick-fast!

Once you call him back after making him wait for your phone call, you'll need to explain how "right back" turned into twenty-four hours later. Tell him that you're sorry you ended the conversation abruptly, but you suddenly remembered you had to call a girlfriend about plans for the night. Then explain you got sidetracked and you just remembered that you forgot to call him back. This brilliant technique works in two ways: First, he will realize right off the bat that you are confident, cool, and a challenge. Second, he will be shocked that the reason you interrupted your phone call in the first place was for a measly conversation with a girlfriend. Not because you left the oven on and your place was burning down, or because you suddenly remembered it was your dad's sixtieth birthday. Chitchat with your girlfriend? Pretty frustrating, borderline amusing, and *very* ballsy. It will secretly annoy him that you treated him like crap.

The result of your very simple plan? In true guy fashion, he will view your dismissive behavior as a challenge and respond by pursuing you even harder.

TIP #3

Block Your Phone Number

■

**Restricting your phone number isn't
just for prank calls anymore.**

The phone can be a very dangerous weapon. Don't let its small size or girlie rings fool you: It is just as deadly as an ATM in a casino. And just like a weapon, it can cause excruciating pain, deep wounds, scarring—even jail time or late-night trips to the ER. Without ample self-restraint it can easily lead you down a dark path of drunk dials, overtime charges, and the temptation to fill every idle minute with conversation. With that said, you must be responsible and not let your poor phone etiquette ruin your relationship before you even get off the ground.

For starters, always restrict your number when you call your guy. (If you don't know how to do this, ask your service provider. On most phones you dial *67 before the phone number and voilà—anonymity!) No, this isn't so you can do the heavy-breathing thing without him knowing. This is so that if you get his voice mail you can hang up without him knowing that you called. The last thing you want is for him to check his phone and see three missed calls from you and no messages. That'll make you look like you're needy, or some kind of stalker, or both. When guys sit around describing their ideal woman the conversation sounds more like, "She has to be hot, independent, smart, funny, and tolerant of my addiction to football" and less like, "She has to be hot, funny, and totally dependent on me for everything, and cling to my side like a bad rash. And if she stares at me while I sleep, that's cool, too." Multiple missed calls are a great way to promote yourself from Private Nonchalant to Lieutenant Psycho.

So you restrict your number and call—only to get his voice mail! Suddenly your palms begin to sweat and a thousand stupid things you could say start racing through your head. What should you do? Be funny, or sexy, or mysterious? No, no, and no. First, take a deep breath, put down the Prozac, and *hang up the phone.* Don't leave a voice mail, not today, not until you've gone out a few times.

There are two main reasons for this: One, if you leave him a message you'll be waiting and waiting and obsessing, I mean waiting, for him to call you back. Keep the ball in your court by letting him wait for your next call. Remember, anticipation is a good thing.

Reason two is that most unrehearsed voice mails sound like this: "Hey, Troy, what's up? It's Lisa . . . and . . . I was just calling to say hi and see what you're up to. Just see what's going on and stuff. So, uh, give me a call when you have the chance and, um, I'll talk to you then. Okay? Cool, OK, talk to you soon. Okay, bye." This is the kind of message I imagine boy band stars get from giggly groupies. He's not Justin Timberlake and you're not fourteen. Spare yourself the embarrassment and hang up before the sound of the tone.

TIP #4

It's Your Dirty Laundry, Not His

■

**Remember: He's a guy, not your best gal pal.
So save your deepest, darkest secrets for
the flight back from the honeymoon.**

Let's have fun with a little scenario: It's Saturday night and you find yourself a couple of drinks into a great date with the new guy you've been seeing. As the conversation progresses you feel yourself wanting to confess something very personal to him. He has after all, shown himself to be very caring. You think it'll be a good move, showing him you like him enough to let him into your private life, so what should stop you? Well, for starters, how about the fear of dying alone? Or maybe just never seeing this Mr. Right again. One or both can happen.

Keep it nice and light. Guys don't want to start lugging around your emotional baggage two months into a relationship. Plain and simple, they won't. I don't care how great you think it will be to open up to him; you've gotta keep the skeletons where they belong—way back in the closet behind the piles of baggy jeans you're convinced will someday make a comeback.

You see, the main problem with this type of heartfelt confession is that guys hear, and therefore interpret, things differently than women. Even though what you're saying isn't awful or inappropriate, he'll think it is.

Let's go back to that date you were on with your new guy. Things are going well so you figure now's a good time to open up to him. You say, "When I was young my dad cheated on my mom and ruined their marriage, so I've always had a hard time trusting guys." He hears, "I'm going to keep extremely close tabs on you and second-guess your intentions routinely." And without fail, this leads him to think, "Hmm, I wonder what my ex is doing later tonight?" And poof! Yet another potentially great guy is heading for the hills. Keep the bad childhood and Freudian analysis out of the conversation and you'll keep him interested. It's not therapy, it's a date.

Guys *do* want to hear you say things like:
- "I never take an hour to get ready." (Translation: "I'm much more low-maintenance than your ex-girlfriend.")
- "Staying in shape is really important to me." (Translation: "I won't gain twenty pounds two years into our relationship.")
- "My last boyfriend was way too clingy." (Translation: "I won't call and bug you ten times a day.")

Guys *don't* want to hear you say things like:
- "My ex and I were inseparable." (Translation: "Say goodbye to your guy friends.")
- "I don't really like to party." (Translation: "The next time you'll be drunk is at your bachelor party.")
- "I'm so over the whole dating game." (Translation: "This finger's looking for a ring, babe.")

Aside from not wanting to take on your personal baggage, guys want to think of you as being perfect for as long as possible (or until you reveal otherwise).

And this doesn't just apply to your emotional state. Don't reveal information about your finances that may make him run for the hills. He doesn't need to know that your credit cards are maxed out and that between your two Visa cards and one American Express, you owe $18,000. Especially when you tell him this information with a chuckle and a nonchalant, "Whatever, I'll pay them off some day." Also, revealing you still have $35,000 worth of student loans to pay off is not good. When you make statements like these, what he really hears is, "If we get married one day, you're going to have pay off all my debt. Want another beer?"

Another nugget of information you want to avoid sharing is anything to do with being in trouble with a government agency. If you "slightly cheated" on your tax returns two years ago and just received an audit letter from the IRS, talk to your parents about that, not the new guy. He doesn't need to know that your "slightly shady" behavior could potentially get him thrown in jail one day, at least not on your second date.

Think about it. A guy opening up about his checkbook and his credit report on the second date is pretty unheard of. And the ones who do are probably in some major debt and looking for a girl to help get them out of it—or at least let them crash at her place for a few months. If that's the case, you don't want this guy, even if he is cute in that dirty, bad-boy way.

TIP #5

Have Aspirations and Career Goals

∎

**A guy never says, "When I grow up, I just
wanna be a husband and a stay-at-home dad."**

Have a goal in life. And no, being pregnant and barefoot does *not* count. Don't get me wrong, I'm not knocking pregnancy or motherhood. I'm sure they're both fantabulous!

What I'm saying is that when a guy asks what your goals for the future are, have aspirations outside of motherhood: a successful career, traveling the world, or even helping the less fortunate. You can't go wrong so long as your aspirations show that you're looking to lead a life outside of the home. Make your life sound interesting, fast-paced, and stressful. Not only will he be interested but he'll think that you might be too busy to make time for him, which he will view as a challenge. And as we know:

GUY + CHALLENGE = GIRL + (ATTENTION + GIFTS + AFFECTION)

But I know you're thinking, "Sure Giuliana, that's easy for you to say. You host an international television show, drive a cushy Escalade on 20s, and hobnob with celebs all day long. What about me? I work in the accounts receiving department at a veterinary supply company and my only future plan is to take advantage of the senior-citizen discount at the movies when I turn fifty-five." First off, big ups to me for being able to read your mind. Thank you, thank you. And second, they're 22s, not 20s, but whose counting? And lastly, you raise a good point because your job and future plan are like boredom on steroids multiplied by infinity.

Here's the quick fix: Lie. Yes, I know that honesty is supposed to be the best policy, but the person who made that up was already married, so they weren't considering the whole "dying alone" factor. You need a man and men want an amazing woman, so find the middle ground by either creating new future plans or embellishing your current ones. For example, if you're planning on spending the next ten years studying the plants in your garden, stretch it a little and tell him that you're interested in exotic plants and planning a trip to a remote rain forest to do research. Or, if you're planning on knitting the world's largest afghan and then having kids . . . well in this case you'll definitely want to flat-out lie. Say you're an ex–FBI field agent and now you're focusing on mastering multiple martial arts. Yes, it's random but it will get you a lot more mileage than labeling yourself the queen of knitting.

TIP #6

Don't Take an Hour to Get Ready

■

Unless you're knitting the scarf you're wearing tonight, you should never take more than forty-five minutes to get ready when your man is waiting for you in the other room.

It's Friday night and you've got a date with a new guy that you really want to impress. After all, he's the first guy you've met in months who didn't graduate at the top of jerk class. So you decide to go all out and start getting ready at lunchtime so that when he gets to your place at seven, you're ready to knock him dead. Good for you—primp yourself out and let him have it. I know you may be thinking, "Wait a second, the tip says not to take an hour to get ready. This psycho just took seven. What gives?"

The deal is this: If the guy isn't waiting on you or watching you get ready, it doesn't matter how long you take. If he picks you up and asks how long it took, say thirty minutes. (That's pretty accurate if you're doing the math in dog years.) The point is, guys love low-maintenance girls. If your flat iron is the reason he's an hour late to a party, you can rest assured he's going to label you high-maintenance and seriously reconsider taking you out again.

Think about it: Would *you* want to date a guy who constantly kept you waiting while he gelled his spiky hair into perfect formation? I don't care how forgiving you are of the whole metrosexual trend; even that would turn you off after a while. There are only so many times you can say, "Sorry we're late. Chad had to refrost his tips. How was the ceremony?" Pretty soon, you'll be giving him and his perfect hair the old "we're through." It's no different for guys: They want a girl who looks great but not at the price of two hours of preparation. They could have spent that time watching an entire football game! Six innings of baseball! Four *Seinfeld* reruns! Not cool.

I realize there are some women who truly believe they need two hours to get ready. In this case I recommend always planning ahead so that you have plenty of alone time before getting together. For example, rather than filling your Saturday afternoon with annoying errands, space your day out so that you have at least a couple of hours of downtime before going out. If he asks why you're home or why you can't hang with him, come up with some excuse about a needy friend, work, or even family. Please do not mention your massive prep routine.

It's inevitable that at some point in the relationship he's going to discover your marathon mirror time. I recommend holding off on letting him find this out for as long as possible; by the time he does, you want him to be way too attached to you to break up. If that doesn't work and he still wants to break up? Tell him you're pregnant.

Just kidding. Ditch the flat iron and earn his respect, as well as the label MY HOT LOW-MAINTENANCE GIRLFRIEND, by keeping your mirror time to a minimum.

TIP #7

Don't Overaccessorize

When putting together your outfit, remember that less means more. More ogling, more conversation, more free drinks . . .

I was recently at a bar and saw a girl who looked like she had been jumped by the accessory rack at Bloomingdale's. She had on four layered necklaces, two wood bracelets, six gold bangles, more rings than an entire rap video, one oversized purely decorative leather belt, a belly chain, a French acrylic manicure and pedicure accompanied by airbrushed diamonds on her index finger, a gold anklet (which complemented her totally original dolphin tattoo—hello, spring break!), and not one but two toe rings. And that's just what I could fit on the bar napkin I originally wrote this on—the list is actually much longer.

This poor girl didn't look bad. Bad would be if she had worn only half of the accessories. Oh no, she looked much worse than bad. Her look is best described as bad C-list celebrity fashion meets *Playboy TV*. In fact, I doubt even horny Pam Anderson fans would have hit on her. Ouch.

I asked myself what on earth would make this poor girl think she looked good. Sure, it could have something to do with the fact that she was double-fisting cosmos, but unless she was drunk when she got dressed, that wouldn't explain it. Utterly perplexed, I decided I had to confront her. After making small chitchat, I saw my chance and said, "Wow, you're definitely the queen of accessories. Look at you go." To which she replied, "Yeah, I know. Don't accessories rock? I wish I could wear, like, a million of them at once." Apparently she was too drunk to count because she was easily wearing over a million.

Initially I thought that overaccessorizing was a trick employed by really skinny girls to keep them anchored to the ground in case of a strong gust of wind. However, my terribly tacky new friend had proved me wrong. Apparently, some women think that since one accessory can accentuate an outfit, then 155 accessories will really make it "rock." Rock? Wrong! Overaccessorizing is a *huge* no-no. Think about it: When you see a guy in the gym wearing a bandana, two wristbands (which match his knit cap), and a utility belt that holds his phone, MP3 player, Palm Pilot, and breath mints, what do you think? L-A-M-E. Or maybe T-O-O-L. Either way, it spells out bad impression.

Another disadvantage with overaccessorizing is the risk you run of appearing obsessed with material things, more specifically, jewelry. After a while even the densest guys will notice your crazy thing for bling. And that could make him think you are way too into material things and that if you two get married one day, you will spend all the money—I mean, *his* money—on jewelry and clothes.

So trust me on this one. Don't be that girl covered in trinkets. Just keep it simple. Jeans and a T-shirt will always grab more attention than a slew of accessories. Don't get me wrong, accessories will get you attention, but it will be in the form of snickers and jeers, and "She's so cheesy!" Get the right kind of attention by limiting the bracelets and other goodies. Guys won't be distracted by the extra bells and whistles and will notice you. And to most men, nothing is hotter than a girl in a T-shirt, jeans, and Chuck Taylors. And if you are dying to show off your new tight pants and sequin halter with your 3½-inch Guccis, fine, but don't wear that outfit to the movies! Guys can get really turned off when they come to pick you up for an eight o'clock flick and you walk out the door in a hoochie-mama outfit. Club, maybe. Movie, no!

Still confused? Imagine this: You see a guy wearing cool jeans and a T-shirt. He's naturally hot and oozes sexy without trying at all. Now, imagine another guy who's gone way too far. He is trying so hard to make you think it didn't take him hours to get ready. In actuality, it took him hours: a three o'clock hair appointment, a four o'clock mani/pedi, a five-fifteen eyebrow wax, a spray tan, a trip to three stores at the mall, and two hours in front of his bathroom and bedroom mirrors. His jeans are factory-faded instead of naturally worn. His concert T-shirt is not an original—the Barneys New York tag gives that one away. As if that's not bad enough, the T-shirt is clearly two sizes too small, so an excessive amount of muscle is popping out all over the place. Then there are the too-new, overly shiny black leather boots and the perfectly slicked-back hair that looks like it was styled with shoe polish. Let's not forget the perfectly arched eyebrows (yuck!) and manicured hands. It's one thing for a guy to have clean nails, but it's a whole other thing when his nails are more manicured than yours. And wait, is that clear nail polish? And just when you thought things couldn't get worse, he's wearing a chunky silver bracelet and a leather necklace with some sort of shark's tooth dangling off the end of it. Surely this is a memento from that "insane" trip he took to the Bahamas with the boys back in 2001. I'll be right back. I'm going to throw up.

TIP #8

Don't Be a Finicky Eater

No onions, no tomatoes, no dressing, no second date.

It's one thing to ask for dressing on the side, but it's another issue altogether when your special order reads longer the original recipe itself. Nobody likes to listen to someone rattle off a laundry list of special requests or reasons for why you can't have carbs, or sodium, or any sort of flavor. Don't put your date through this painful ordeal. Either learn to eat like a regular person or take the initiative and pick a restaurant where you know you can order off the menu. Not only will you be able to order easily, but he'll appreciate the fact that you were decisive and he didn't have to plan everything.

If you are a neurotic eater, avoid showing him that side of you at all costs for the first several dates. Unless of course he's a ballet dancer or a male model. (Actually, I once dated a male model and he was a pig—a lot of them are just gorgeous and blessed with a superfast metabolism. Bastards.) But unless your new guy is on a strict diet, don't tell him you are really anal when it comes to food. A guy wants a girl who will be able to eat at his favorite spots, including the baseball game and gas station, from time to time. If he finds out that you only eat at the all-natural, all-organic restaurant on the other side of town he's going to seriously reconsider calling you again. It's too much work for him to constantly have to cater to your fickle dietary needs. The only time picky eating is acceptable is if you're pregnant. But then again, if you're pregnant, your finicky eating will be the least of his worries.

This tip is not just limited to solids. Learn to love simple coffee drinks as well. Don't go into a crowded Starbucks and order your double, tall, caramel, half-caf, extra foam, nonfat latte with a shot of sugar-free vanilla and two Splendas. By the time you're at extra foam your guy is already off sharing a normal latte with a normal girl. Unless you're in the mood for a venti serving of solitude, leave the complex coffee orders to the diehard coffee junkies.

Even if you're not a finicky eater, there are going to be times when you can't eat certain foods, like when you go on a diet right before summer or your sister's wedding. In case of a diet the best way to avoid annoying your guy is to just tell him what you can't eat and offer up some alternatives. Make dealing with your diet simple for him, the easier the better. Rather than going to an Italian restaurant and saying no to everything he suggests off the menu, tell him before you go out that you're on a high-protein diet, so how about trying a steak house? Aged filet mignon? *Good*. High-maintenance carb-aphobe girlfriend? *Bad*.

TIP #9

Don't Model Yourself After Paris Hilton

Unless you're worth $250 million, the sexy heiress act isn't going to get you very far.

Quick identity check: Can you write the following sentence in cursive? "I am Paris Hilton and that's hot!" You did it? Congratulations! You're not Paris Hilton.

I'll admit it's hard not to envy Paris Hilton every now and again. She's on the cover of every magazine, she's got a hit show, she's hot enough to make a hamburger commercial sexy, and she's known throughout the world. Oh, and she's worth more money than you could spend in a lifetime. Not too shabby.

However, don't let your envy take you to the point of trying to become Paris. Why? Because at the end of the day she is famous and filthy rich, so everyone tolerates her ridiculous behavior. You, on the other hand, are neither rich nor a celebrity. This means that your fake tan, bleached-blond hair, and constant repetition of "That's hot!" will have you looking more like a sorority spring-breaker than a Hollywood A-lister.

While it's a bit of a stretch, think of it this way: What would you think of a guy who modeled himself after Fabio? Forget about the fame and money. Just imagine you're in bar and a guy with frosted tips, a fake tan, eyeliner, and catchphrases like "Ciao, bella" approached you. Surely you would laugh in his face. Fabio gets away with lame catchphrases and the cheesiest appearance on the planet because he's a celebrity. He's on TV, romance book covers, and billboards. He's not a mere human, and as a result he's not held to our tips and customs.

Except for hard-core metros, most guys don't think that if they dress and act like Fabio, they'll get more girls. But metros don't count because they really don't care what women think so long as other metros check them out. Real guys may embellish one thing that Fabio does, like fake tanning or waxing unwanted body hair, but they don't undergo a complete makeover. The same tip should apply to women. If you really love Paris, then maybe try wearing your hair like hers or fake-tan yourself, but don't go overboard. And whatever you do, don't ever carry around a tiny dog in your purse. It's like having a cold sore but worse, because unlike a cold sore a guy can spot that doggie-purse combo a mile away and run before you can say hi.

Matt, age twenty-seven, Seattle

Recently a friend of mine set me up on a blind date. I usually shy away from setups, but I figured it couldn't hurt to give it a shot this time. I was wrong. The date quickly became one of the most (if not *the* most) painful dates of my life. I arrived at the restaurant early, was seated at my table, and was eventually (yes, *eventually*— she was monumentally, not fashionably, late, strike one) met by a fairly attractive woman, who on the surface didn't resemble Paris Hilton, but as I would come to realize had the air of Paris, which is a hundred times worse than looking like Paris.

While I don't know her, the only uses I could ever imagine for the celeb-utante would be:

1. Sleep with her. (We've all seen the tape. It looks fun!)
2. Spend her money. (Did I even need to mention this one?)

Aside from that, I can't think of a single redeemable quality in Paris Hilton or a Paris Hilton type. My impression of her is this: shallow, petty, selfish, self-absorbed, and stupid. The worst combination of traits a human being can have.

Moments after she sat down I noticed that her purse moved and then began to whine. Can you guess what was in her purse? That's right, a dog. A dog. She brought her goddamn dog on a blind date?! (Strike two.) It's such an idiotic idea that thinking about it for more than twenty seconds at a time causes me to pass out. Dogs don't belong on dates, nor do they belong in purses.

As if that weren't bad enough, I realized over dinner that she had a crippling addiction to her Sidekick. She would relentlessly and unapologetically type, read messages, and giggle like a retard.

Leave the Sidekick in your purse. I don't give a shit if the dog chews on it. (Strike three.)

Our dinner conversation focused on the most inane shit ever. She could only bring herself to talk about people that I didn't know (strike four), parties that I hadn't been to (strike five), buying clothes—not fashion, mind you, but the actual process of purchasing clothes (I'm not even counting the strikes anymore), and, oh yes, Paris herself came up three or four times (no, she didn't know her). When she wasn't talking she looked like she was purposefully posing, which is distracting and awkward for everyone involved. It's impossible for me to carry on a conversation with someone when half my brain is trying to complete a sentence while the other half is trying figure out why she keeps sucking in her cheeks.

She also went as far as to use the phrase "that's hot" no less than ninety times over the course of the two-hour dinner (that's almost once a minute!). The number of times she said it combo'd with the way she said it just made her sound like an idiot. When a woman says, "That's hot," a little voice inside men says, "Deal breaker!"

My date displayed all of the negative qualities I associate with Paris Hilton and, frankly, she wasn't nearly attractive or wealthy enough to pull it off. Had she been really hot or really wealthy (and let's face it, those are the reasons anyone tolerates the real Paris Hilton), I might have been able to tolerate her long enough to sleep with her and spend her money, but at the end of the night my impression of my date was this: shallow, petty, selfish, self-absorbed, and stupid. ■

TIP #10

Don't Giggle During Sex

And if you do, expect him to
be totally offended.

TIP #11

Don't Cry During Sex

And if you do, expect him to
be scarred for life.

TIP #12

Talk Like a Lady, Not a Trucker

**Peppering every sentence
with a slew of vulgarities isn't
attractive, it's trashy. Copy that, babe?**

Who doesn't love cursing? It's an effective way of conveying an emotion, it makes bad jokes laughable, and, simply put, sometimes it's the only way to get your fuckin' point across. I'm a big advocate of bad language—in moderation. Knowing when and where it's appropriate to drop an F-bomb is a must for anyone planning on adding such gems as "fuckhead" to their vocab. Well-placed swear words can make you look funny and charming. However, as soon as you start making the word "shit" the subject and verb of every sentence, you have a problem. You go from looking like a sharp-tongued hottie to foul-mouthed truck driver, and you know who dates truckers? Other truckers, so curb the trucker-speak.

Those of you who swear about as often as you have a period can ignore this tip. I'm directing this one to the ladies who describe *The Notebook* as "so fucking romantic" and casually refer to exes as "mother-fucking assholes." Yes, this one's for you, Ms. Potty Mouth.

Think about it from a guy's point of view: Would you want to date someone who couldn't get through a movie or a meal without offending several bystanders? No, and neither does your new guy. There are only so many times he'll apologize to the people at the next table ("I'm sorry, she has a mild case of Tourette's") before he'll get tired of consoling crying children and dump you. Look at any quality guy and note how often he swears—excluding at the gym and during sex. Not too often, right? That's because he knows that if he introduces the terms "bitch tits," "fat fuck," and "shit eater" before dessert he may not be getting a second date.

Remember, swear words should be the exception, not the norm. Make like a guy (a quality one, at that) and practice moderation. Introduce him to your bad vocab slowly, giving him just enough to hint at your darker side. After all, having an edge will increase your appeal, unless of course you're dating an Amish man. In that case, you'll want to curb all vulgarities and provocative behavior. And you'll probably want to stop using electricity, too. Come to think of it, it's probably not going to work out between you and brother Ezekiel, so stick to the regular guys and embrace the occasional vulgarity.

TIP #13

Don't Admit You Were a Bad Student

C's may have been enough to earn you a degree, but they're not enough to earn you his respect.

Remember that girl in high school who was class president, started ten clubs, and graduated with a perfect 4.0 GPA? Don't feel bad, no one else remembers that girl either because she spent all of her time studying and attending club meetings. You, like most girls, probably spent more time developing a personality and honing your social skills. So you cut a couple of classes and didn't study quite as much as the dorky kids, so what? Math was never your subject anyway.

Despite Miss 4.0's hard work and your lack thereof, you still walked across the same stage. You just had a few less colorful stripes—no big deal, you never were much for flashy outfits. Now, several years later, you find yourself on a date and your guy asks what kind of student you were. Your knee-jerk reaction is to tell him that you were pretty lousy because you barely had time for school in between concerts and house parties. There doesn't seem to be anything wrong with that; after all, you were the coolest girl in school, right? Wrong. Before you go bragging, remember that you're talking about being cool in a time when Corey Feldman and mullets were cool. In other words, your solid C behavior was kicked off the cool train years ago. Where does that leave you? Somewhere between a 4.0 and a 3.2.

What I'm saying is that if you weren't a good student, pad your GPA a little so that you land somewhere in the A– to B range. I realize that something as trivial as your high school GPA may not be a deal breaker, but it certainly will affect his opinion of you. Think about it: If you were a dating a new guy, would you rather find out that he was homecoming king or king of the keg stand? That he graduated with a 4.0 or at a fourth-grade level? It doesn't take an honor student to figure it out—guys prefer girls with brains.

This tip also applies to the SATs. Never admit you got anything less than a score of 1050. Adjust the score depending on how intelligent the guy you're dealing with is. If he is of just about average intelligence, throw out an 1100. He'll think that's phenomenal! If he's very smart and went to an Ivy League school, you may want to throw out at least a 1200. Forget phenomenal—he'll think that's prodigious. (Remember in the introduction when I said no thesaurus was used in the making of this book? Yeah, well, I take that back. But I promise, "prodigious" is the only time I used a thesaurus while writing this book.)

But what happens when it comes time to prove your GPA and SAT scores to this new guy, you ask? Don't worry about that. He will never try to uncover your true score. And if for some insane reason he asks you for proof, tell him you have no clue where the paperwork is. I mean, who holds on to old SAT results or report cards anyway?

Of course, the same tip applies to college. In fact, here are a couple of good buzz terms to throw around if he asks how you did in college: "cum laude," "magna cum laude," and "summa cum laude." Basically they mean, "I rocked," "I was the shit," and "I was the schizzle fo' rizzle." Two things to note: Unless you have multiple personalities, you can only be one of the terms: for example, "I graduated cum laude," not "I graduated cum laude summa cum laude." Oh, and remember, "cum" is pronounced "koom," like "boom" but with a "K." With that said, when it comes to your scholastic track record stick to the A's and B's. The only C's you should gloat about are the ones he's been staring at all night.

TIP #14

Be Civil When It Comes to Politics

Just because he may one day share your bed doesn't mean he has to share your political beliefs.

You're smart, you're worldly, and you have plenty of educated opinions on the way things should be. Good for you. No, seriously, it's a great thing. By having educated thoughts of your own you've already separated yourself from the millions of girls that don't. Well, they do, but "I'm, like, into reading 'n stuff" doesn't count, so no. However, having opinions is only half the battle. Knowing when and how to convey them is just as important.

Let's take a common issue of debate—political affiliation. Is he a Democrat or a Republican? Let's say that you're on your second date with a guy and as dinner progresses the issue of politics arises. To your dismay you find out that he doesn't sport the same bumper stickers as you, uh-oh. Now there are two ways to handle the situation. One is chosen by the majority of the sane population; the other is reserved for those who enjoy the sound of their own voice.

Scenario one (sane folk) plays out like this: He says he's a Republican. You inform him that you're a Democrat and ask what he likes about his party. Then you can bring up an issue or two and partake in some civil, *mature* (note the italics) debate. Not only will it give you the chance to show off your intellect (which he'll respect), but you may even learn a thing or two. Additionally, sometimes a little heated debate, especially when combined with alcohol, can be a huge turn-on. So first wow him with your outfit and good looks, and then debate your way into a third date.

Scenario two (psychoville) goes like this: He says he's a Republican and you reach over and stab him with your fork while screaming obscenities. Okay, maybe that's just what you think in your head. What really happens is you act betrayed that he could have such a view and then you launch into a "How could you" tirade full of insults and threats that continues long through dessert and coffee. By the time you get off your soapbox, you've broken a sweat and he's ready for intensive group therapy. Suffice to say, a third date is not in the cards.

Here's the deal: Both scenarios ensure that you'll hear from him again. The difference however, lies in the nature of the phone call. In scenario one, he'll be calling to invite you over for wine and more debate. In scenario two, he'll call to inform you that he's taking you to court for the irreparable mental and emotional trauma he suffered at your hands. In that case, vote for scenario one.

TIP #15

Have a Sense of Humor

Knock knock.
Who's there?
Girl with no sense of humor.
Girl with no sense of humor, who?
Girl with no sense of humor who's never going to
keep a guy because she can't take a joke.

In the land of bar conversation the dirty joke reigns supreme. In between beer guzzling, sprints to the bathroom, and shouting at the TV, guys fill the gaps with some of the loudest, most juvenile jokes ever created. They're offensive, dirty, and childish. And really bad, too. The bar is like Pinocchio Island where all the boys go to smoke cigars and play pool, and much like Pinocchio, they eventually turn into jackasses before the evening is over.

But whether you're still looking for a guy or already in a relationship, you're going to have to frequent this island of immaturity. And while you're visiting you're going to have to be able to hang with the guys and roll with the punches. The donkey punches, that is. And the dirty Sanchez. And just about every other dirty phrase and nickname ever invented.

Picture bar time with the guys as a sort of trial by fire. If you can handle their trucker talk and shenanigans, then you'll be respected as a fun girl who can be one of the guys. Being able to be one of the guys will increase the value of your stock considerably. Think of it from a guy's perspective: Would you want to date a girl you couldn't take to hang out with you and your friends? No way. You'd want a girl you wouldn't have to babysit, someone who won't be offended by every dirty joke. Be that easygoing girl.

I'm not saying that you have to actually find humor in every joke or really enjoy them, you just have to learn to laugh at them and not be offended. He doesn't really care if you like the jokes so long as you don't mind them and occasionally laugh at one or two. I'll be the first to admit that most dirty jokes are either immature or stupid. Most are both. But take off your joke critic hat and pretend to enjoy them for the sake of your relationship. Not only will he appreciate your tolerance of their pirate talk, but his friends will be sure to point out that you are so much cooler than their uptight girlfriends. And the award for least likely to be dumped goes to—you. Congratulations.

TIP #16

Don't Obsess Over Babies and Puppies

**Resist the urge to appear too interested
or fascinated with infants. Simply
acknowledge them and move on. Don't get all
mushy over them. Otherwise he'll think
you want to have a baby right now.**

Why is that even well-educated, self-respecting women act like boy band groupies at the sight of a newborn? Not to worry, I don't expect you to have an answer, because if you did, you'd have your own book and wouldn't be reading mine. Book aside, what crazy gene in our DNA causes us to lose control of ourselves in the presence of babies? You take any woman and show her a baby and suddenly it's like she's taken a deep breath of helium and been kicked in the head. The pitch of her voice becomes so high that even dogs' ears begin to bleed and her normally impressive vocabulary is long gone. And with the vocab, gone is the guy she used to call Babe. Or Honey. Or Boo, if she's into the whole hip-hop scene. The point is, her man is gone.

Leave the goo-goo gaga act to the baby. Save your dignity—and the relationship—by holding off on the baby-speak. Spare yourself the embarrassment of admitting to your friends that your relationship bombed because of your out-of-control baby talk.

Therefore, when out in public, *do not* let your boyfriend catch you showering a baby with high-pitched babblery. He will draw two conclusions: One, you are way too baby-friendly, and perhaps dying to have your own offspring. And two, if that's the way you talk to a baby you don't know, just think how badly you're going to baby-talk *him* after a couple of months. He'll be gone before you can say, "I love you, my little-wittle boo-boo-head."

I'm not saying that you should be mean to babies. But don't go out of your way to be incredibly nice to them, either. Be cordial, especially when their parents are watching. Don't make a production out of the experience. Acknowledge the child, maybe compliment the parents on how cute it is—after all, they spent nine months waiting for the thing; the least you could do is throw them a bone—and move on. If you really want to be slick, you can tell your guy something like, "You know, babies are great and all, but I just couldn't imagine having one right now." This lets him know that you're not a heartless robot (FYI, robots hate kids), yet at the same time, you're not racing to be a mommy with four kids climbing all over her like she's a jungle gym.

So the next time you're standing in line with your guy at the grocery store and there's a couple in front of you holding a baby, *do not* start fawning all over the baby, no matter how chubby its cheeks are or how big and blue its eyes are. Instead, turn your back—yes, turn your back to the child and strike up a conversation about the weather with your man. Even if the baby is doing that thing some babies do. You know—when they make eye contact with you and start giggling and reaching out to you. Almost like they have some sixth sense that's telling them that you are dying to have a baby. I know it's heartless, but don't acknowledge that cute little gaze. Don't reach out for those pudgy little arms. *Turn your back, woman!* The baby will get over it in two seconds flat, and your man will subconsciously realize that you are with him because you want to be, not because you are just dying to find a husband and procreate.

Baby talk, bad. Got that, pookie?

Never, Ever Kiss on the First Date

■

**Leave him with a lasting impression,
not lipstick on the collar.**

He shows up at your place looking like he jumped off the cover of *GQ* and takes you to an amazing Italian restaurant in the kind of Mercedes you only see in rap videos. Impressive, but it's not over yet. He orders a bottle of Dom and begins showering you with compliments, one after another, until you're barely able to keep yourself from jumping across the table and reenacting that scene from *The Thomas Crown Affair.* But you hold strong and manage to make it through the meal without tackling him. The check comes and goes and before you know it you're back in his mobile rap video on the way back to your house. In true gentleman fashion he opens your door, gives you his hand, and walks you to your front door.

And then what? Do you let yourself be swept away by the moment and kiss him? Yes, hooker, you do. Then you take him inside, have passionate, conjugal-visit style sex, and then marry him, because clearly you're dating either Bruce Wayne or James Bond. But in all other cases you should say good night and leave him standing on the porch wondering why you didn't kiss him. Why? Because you *never* kiss on the first date.

Listen to me, no matter how great a time you have on the first date, you have to resist temptation and deny him a kiss. It will drive him nuts. He'll run through all the possible reasons why you didn't kiss him: Are you not into him? Did he do something wrong? Do you ever kiss on the first date? Are you actually, really, one of those impossible-to-find good girls? His mental frustration is your gain because in the end he'll need to see you again and figure out what the reason is. Guys are stubborn and don't take rejection easily. Ironically enough, they want what they can't have. Reject him. Not just once—do it often. What the hell, make a habit of it. Sure he'll be frustrated, but he'll respect you for it, and as a result every little morsel of affection you give him will be that much more precious and appreciated.

TIP #18

*Words Never to Mention on
the First Three Dates*

■

SOULMATE   REHAB

DESTINY

BABY   DISEASE

WEDDING

MY SISTER'S WEDDING   ASTROLOGY

THERAPIST   PROZAC

RESTRAINING ORDER

EX-HUSBAND

BIOLOGICAL CLOCK

TIP #19

Avoid a Purely Textual Relationship

Abuse of text messaging may turn a wonderful sexual relationship into a purely textual one.

There are several four-letter words that classy women should limit using. Sadly, "text" is one of them. Text messaging ("texting") is something kids in junior high and high school do when they're bored in class. There's no reason for you to be texting your new guy, even if he has the maturity of an eighteen-year-old and still wears his letterman's jacket. On second thought, if your guy still wears his letterman's jacket you may want to consider making him your ex-guy. Seriously, wearing a letterman's jacket is like wearing parachute pants, a Members Only jacket, or a rhinestone glove, or all of the above. Come on, you don't want to be known as the girl who dated the guy trapped in 1985.

Back to the issue at hand: Texting is bad. It's childish, time-consuming, and, when done in public, quite embarrassing. It's like stuttering. Suddenly a two-minute conversation takes ten and everything that makes face-to-face conversations interesting is gone. Flirtatious smiles and laughs are replaced with symbols so lame that even nerds shy away from using them—rather than seeing your beautiful smile when you laugh he gets :) and your sly, sexy wink becomes ;)—dry humor and sarcasm are misinterpreted as genuine stupidity or rudeness, and any chance of spontaneity or chemistry is gone. Oh, and let us not forget that the male attention span ranges from three to five seconds, so the chances of him actually reading and then responding to your epic text messages are slim.

However, from time to time the text message comes in quite handy. Like if you don't want to explain to a guy why you can't see him tonight (for some reason "A much hotter guy invited me out" doesn't go over well), a text is the perfect way to handle the situation. There's no awkward conversation, no excuses, no drama. Just be responsible and only use text messages when necessary.

Don't *ever* send a message just to say hi. I swear that if I catch another one of my friends texting a guy with "Hey hottie, just saying hi," I'm going to throw her phone into a raging river and then jump in right behind it. A bubbly text message isn't the mark of maturity or intelligence. It says you're bored. Guys aren't interested in girls who are bored or boring—they want mystery and excitement.

How is "I was just thinking of you and wanted to say hi!" not the lamest, least racy comment you've ever heard? Perfect grammar, excellent syntax, and you even included an exclamation point. Wow. Do you know what *muuuuggghh* is? It's my attempt at capturing the sound I make when I throw up in my mouth, which is what I do every time I read a stupid text message. Please, save your relationship and my lunch—no more bad text messages.

These days guys especially are getting waaaay too comfortable with their little BlackBerry, replacing the telephone as their main form of making plans with you and checking in with you throughout the day. If you're not careful, your guy can go days, even weeks, without ever having a phone conversation with you, yet he ends up in your bed three times a week. Hey, how'd he do that? His BlackBerry and your lack of self-respect, that's how! Texting should be a supplement to the relationship, not the basis of one. If a guy wants to ask you to dinner and a movie on Saturday night, he should call and ask you. If a guy wants to tell you he'll be over in ten minutes to pick you up for your hot date, he can text you. See the difference? If you don't establish this early in the relationship, then before you know it, his sexy chuckle will be replaced by LOL. Trust me, if he really wants to get to know you and is legitimately interested in you, he'll like to hear your voice and make the effort to talk to you.

TIP #20

Periods Shouldn't Suck

■

When you have your period or a medical condition that prevents you from fooling around, don't reveal it. Instead, use Mother Nature's intrusion as an opportunity to blow him off for the night. It'll keep him interested and unaware of your condition.

Honesty is a good thing and more often than not it is the best policy. However, when it comes to letting your new guy know that you have your period, steer as far from the truth as possible. I don't care what kind of honesty pact you and he entered into, it is in the best interest of the relationship to keep him oblivious to your little ailment. Ignorance is bliss and menstruation is unsexy. Period. No pun intended.

There's no reason for you to ever tell a guy you're casually dating that you have your period. In no way do you benefit by sharing this tidbit of information. He'll just think "ew" or "gross" or some variation of the two. He certainly won't think, "Damn that's hot!" or "Geez, she's so real, I love it." Telling him the truth is a lose-lose situation.

Guys want you to be sexy, mysterious, and different from all the other girls they've dated. Don't give him any reason to think otherwise. When your period comes up, use it as an opportunity to play the elusive card. When he asks you out, give him the slip and a vague excuse. Tell him you have a "friend" in town for the night that you'll be visiting with. This answer will kill him. If he asks who the friend is, have some fun with him, laugh and say something like, "Why, do I detect a little jealousy?" The more nonchalant you are, the better. By telling him something like this you accomplish a few things:

- He's going to keep thinking about you and what you're really doing. This is great because the more time you're on his mind, the more he's going to be interested in you.
- He's going to think that you may be dating other guys (whether you really are is irrelevant so long as he *thinks* you are). This is great, because if he thinks that several guys are chasing after you, it'll increase your overall appeal in his eyes. Also, if he thinks that several guys are chasing after you, his competitive side will kick in and he'll want to be the one who gets you, which will increase his interest and effort tremendously.
- He's going to think that he's not important enough for the truth (or your time). This will make him chase you even harder. Remember, with guys it's all about the challenge: The less you give them, the more they'll want you.

So unless your physical ailment is something cool or flattering ("I have a wicked hangover from drinking beers at the football game" is a good one), skip the truth, brush him off, and watch his interest grow.

Bad cramps. Heavy flows. Urinary tract infections. Hell, even an ear infection is painful and unsexy. All of the above may keep you from hanging out with your new man a couple of nights, but its worth it. So instead of being up front and honest with your boyfriend, it's better to seize the fact that you are out of commission. It's a great opportunity to seem aloof, without telling him why you really can't see him. Period.

TIP #21

Items to Take Out of Your Medicine Cabinet

Yeast infection cream
Antidepressants
Facial hair wax strips
Bladder infection pills
Bulk-size pack of Fleet enemas
Prescription painkillers
Hemorrhoid cream
Pregnancy tests
Anything with the "Summer's Eve" label

TIP #22

F and Run,
aka
Pull a Coyote

■

**Make a quick escape the morning after
your first few sleepovers. Don't bug him to
take you to brunch. Head for the door, not
Rooty Tooty Fresh and Fruity.**

You've been there before. You open your eyes to the bright morning sun expecting to catch a glimpse of your expensive armoire. Instead you are startled at the sight of an IKEA nightstand with a large digital clock that reads 8:06 A.M. You blink. You blink again and again, thinking that surely on the fourth or fifth blink, you will open your eyes to the sight of your cell phone sitting on your nightstand right next to your magazines. Blink, blink, blink, blink, blink. Nope. The black, obnoxiously large digital alarm clock is still there. Only now it's blinking 8:07 A.M. and you realize you are in the cute-guy-from-last-night's bed. Before you waste another minute *run, do not walk, to the nearest exit!*

OK, you can't exactly run—you'll look like a psycho. But you

do need to think fast. Here's what you do. Instead of risking waking up the hottie to the left, listen for snoring, even breathing,
coming from the other side of the bed. Hear it? OK, good. Now
the difficult part kicks in. Difficult because most women, needy
creatures that we are, instinctually want to roll over, nuzzle right
up to Mr. Hottie's backside, and spoon. We want so badly to cuddle for the next hour, chitchat and giggle with this adorable guy
who swept us off our feet in the wee hours of the morning. Then
we want to hop out of bed and hop into Boy's car and cruise over
to the yummy brunch spot down the street and pig out on pancakes, eggs, and a couple cups of coffee. Sounds great, huh? Well
the truth is, you think it's great and as a matter of fact . . . he
probably does too! I know you thought I was gonna say he'd hate
it, but in fact, he would love to chow down with the hot girl from
the night before. So what's the problem, you ask? Here, let me
spell it out for you.

T-O-O E-A-S-Y! Yes, too easy. What you need to do is quietly get out of bed, grab your clothes off the floor (don't forget
your bra in the living room!), and get the f— out of there! Don't
purposely trip or fake-cough or rattle papers, hoping he will
wake up and convince you to stay. Pull a coyote if you must.

I would write out the definition of the word "coyote," but the
dictionary term does not apply in this particular case. "Pulling a
coyote" is what you do when you are trying to leave a guy's bed
but can't because you are wedged between the pillow and his
arm. Instead of waiting for him to move, you make like a coyote
and start gnawing your arm off to escape his killer grip. OK, obviously you're not literally going to gnaw off your arm—it's more
of a figurative way to describe your need to get the hell out of
there.

Therefore, let him cuddle with you first. Let him suggest
brunch first. If you sense he's being even the slightest bit dis-
tant right when you guys wake up or right after sex, you should

pole-vault out of bed and pretend you have somewhere to go or someone to meet. Even if he insists that you stay, you should bail the first couple of times you spend the night. So much cooler than lingering.

Listen, if you bail against his wishes, he will be thinking so much more about you than if you'd stayed. He'll be asking himself, "Did I do something wrong?" "Did she not like me?" "Did my messy apartment chase her away?" The guy will dwell all day on what caused you to just up and leave him, especially since he felt the two of you shared a wonderful night. That morning, when he goes to brunch with his friends, he most definitely will tell them all about the night before and that morning. He'll joke around, "Can you believe it, she just bailed quick-fast! No note, no good-bye, no nothing." His friends will be amazed and they will all think you are so cool for ditching this guy—most girls latch onto him the morning after.

Trust me, you'll get much more respect from his friends than the last girl he brought to the "morning-after" brunch. The one who showed up at the busy pancake house with ratty hair and smeared eyeliner, wearing her hoochie clothes from the night before "camouflaged" under an oversized men's sweatshirt. Did they mention she smelled like cheap booze? Yuck! See, if you play it right, you will look golden the next morning, and you will be the topic of conversation, in a good way. And even though he and his friends will be trying to downplay the fact that you seriously dissed him that morning, he will keep questioning himself for the rest of the day. "Was I not cool enough for her?" "Was I not good enough?" "Will she ever call me again?"

This scenario is starting to sound oddly familiar, isn't it? That's because this sort of thing happens to girls all the time! Suddenly, the tables have turned and the guy is more in the girl's role. It's a total role reversal. Men customarily do this to girls—hit the sack and run the next morning never to be heard from again. But not this time! That's because you left on the up side, on a good note. You left with the ball in your court.

Quick science lesson before we wrap this up. I hated science too, but this will help explain why you have that urge to latch on to him after fooling around or having sex. One word—oxytocin. Do you know what oxytocin is? No, not the poor man's heroin—that's OxyContin. Anyway, oxytocin is a hormone both men and women release while having sex. And when it's released, it heightens our emotions. Our desire to love shoots through the roof, as does our desire to nest. These emotions occur in the woman as well as the man. The difference is men have something called testosterone, which actually counteracts the effect oxytocin has on their bodies. Women have nothing to counteract it. Therefore, after sex, *we* are dying for the guy to pull us toward him and cradle us in his arms while talking about growing old together and baby names. *He* is wondering what time the gym closes.

So what do you do? Well, first you have to realize that nothing you do will change the way men are wired. You have to just let nature take its course. And since there's no use trying to change him, you yourself have to take action.

The more mysterious a guy is, the more you like him, right? Do the same. Remain a mystery.

Billy, age twenty-four, Miami

I always thought of myself as a guy that was different from most other guys. Unlike most men, I was never one to F and run if I really liked the girl. I haven't had a lot of girls leave me in the middle of the night, either. I liked to spend the morning, maybe even the day, together. I always found something romantic about lounging around till noon, maybe even sharing a toothbrush once in a while. But to be honest, I don't remember much of those mornings or days now. What do I remember? The time I was left alone . . . in the middle of the night.

The first time it ever happened to me, I remember waking up the morning after a really great date followed by really fun sex. I opened my eyes to see the right side of my bed empty. I got out of bed, expecting to find her in my living room, on my couch, in one of my shirts, reading a magazine, but no. She was nowhere to be found. I looked on my coffee table for a note—nothing. I looked in my bathroom, on my kitchen counter, on my nightstand. I even looked in my bed, thinking that she may have left it on the pillow and it had somehow gotten lost in my sheets. Nothing. I was dumbfounded.

I have to admit that being left like that did quite a number on me for most of the day. I tried to play it off, even to myself, like I wasn't bothered by it, but inside it drove me crazy. All day she was all I could think about. "What did I do?" I asked myself "What should I have done differently?" "Did I snore?" "Was she grossed out by my apartment?" and the one that almost drove me over the edge: "Did she not have as much fun as I did last night?" The more I doubted myself, the more I found myself thinking about her and romanticizing what the day would have been like if she had stayed.

Just before I thought I couldn't take it anymore and picked up the phone to find out what happened, she called. She said she just had some errands to run but wanted to see me again. After a day of self-doubt, I now felt like I was invincible. I suppose absence makes the heart grow fonder because I couldn't wait for our next date. I planned all of the things we would do the morning after and when it finally came . . . I woke up alone. It wasn't until the fourth time she slept over that I woke up to find her next to me. Let me tell you, I was over the moon. It made that first day we spent together as great as, if not better than, the sex. ▪

TIP #23

Never Admit You've Slept with More Than Five Guys

Telling your guy that you've slept with more than five guys is like telling a child there really is no Santa Claus, or Easter Bunny, or Tooth Fairy, or Heaven. Don't kill the fantasy.

Don't reveal everything about your sex life or how many guys you've slept with—if it's over five, lie. Why? Aside from all the machismo, five o'clock shadow, and deer hunting, men really are delicate creatures. Once you get past the tough talk and Bowflex-enhanced exterior, most guys are the same person with a few requirements. One of these requirements is the knowledge that the girl they're dating is special. They need to feel a sense of accomplishment at having landed such a difficult catch, and ladies, I'm sorry to tell you, but a big part of your allure is the number of men you've slept with before him.

A *low* number tells him that you're very selective in your partners, and getting you into bed will be a challenge. Guys love challenges, and as an extension of this, they will love chasing you.

A *high* number says many things, including but not limited to the following:

- We're definitely going to run into guys I've slept with when we go out.
- When you tell your friends who you're dating, their reaction will be something along the line of "Awww, shit, do I *know* her!" (*high fives to the surrounding guys*) or "Oh, you're dating *her*." (*awkward silence*) "I mean, sure, I think I've heard her name before." (*more awkward silence*)
- My name is tattooed on several frat boys' arms (right beneath the barbed-wire tattoo).
- I'm unable to keep a guy interested with my personality alone so I compensate by putting out immediately.
- What were you for Halloween? I was a slut. Oh wait, that wasn't Halloween, that was last Tuesday. And Wednesday. And Thursday . . .

The explanation is long-winded but the moral is short: Keep the number of partners below five. I don't care if it's twenty-five. When he asks, it's four. If he questions your response or seems skeptical, take the opportunity to make yourself look good by saying something about how you don't sleep with just any guy you're dating. If you're going to sleep with someone, he needs to be special. This is just one example of what you could say. Really, anything that indicates a high level of self-respect on your part will keep him interested.

TIP #24

Don't Be a Slut in Bed

**Don't act too experienced in the bedroom.
Make him feel like he's the first to introduce
you to different positions and sex games.**

There is a misconception in the world of women that men like girls who know how to screw like porn stars. This is true if a guy is looking for a short-term chick to drive him wild in the bedroom, with no intention of ever letting the girl get past the bedroom. In fact, he has no intention of ever seeing the light of day with this girl. He'll never go out in public with her, and he definitely won't ever introduce her to his friends or family. She's simply his "Sunday night sushi." Quick, no atmosphere, easy, at the end of the week, with Friday and Saturday nights reserved for taking out girls who command a certain degree of respect.

So if you've been around the block a few times (many girls have, no need to be ashamed), simply reserve that information for yourself and a few of your girlfriends. This all comes back to the "Never, ever, ever tell a guy you've slept with more than five guys" tip. Remember, even if the guy admits he's slept with a ton of girls, and even if the guy insists you can tell him the truth, that he won't judge you—never, ever, ever admit to over five! If you ever admit to more than five guys, he will dwell on it until his dying day. He may picture dozens of nameless faces while the two of you make love. Every so often, as he crawls on top of you for a little lovemaking, nasty thoughts may run through his mind: "Ugh, I can't believe thirty guys have been here before me. This girl is nasty!" The truth is, you aren't nasty. You know that, but he doesn't. Even if a guy has slept with a hundred girls and you've slept with twenty guys, it makes no difference to him. He can justify his hundred girls, but he will never feel like you can justify your twenty. So instead of risking a bad reaction, simply keep the truth from him. Rely on the old cliché: What you don't know won't hurt you. Men rely on that cliché at least 50 percent of the time in a relationship, so we should too. OK, enough of this—I just felt that refresher course was necessary and it brings us to my next point.

Back to the actual lovemaking. Remember all those kinky, hot things you learned from the ten or so you guys you really did sleep with? Well, put those skills on hold for a while. In fact, the first time you have sex, don't do anything too kinky. You'll look like a little ho. As a matter of fact, hold on to missionary for as long as possible before giving in to being flipped over and experimenting with other positions, or introducing toys, lotions, gadgets, handcuffs, etc. Whenever he tries kinky stuff, tell him you're embarrassed, or that you're scared, or that it seems "dirty." But make him feel like the more time you spend with him in the bedroom, and the more your relationship evolves, the more open you are to trying new things with him. That's the key—with him! Make him feel like *he's* bringing out the animal in you. That he holds the key to making you lose your inhibitions and get wild in the sack.

Once enough time has passed, start "experimenting" with

him. (I put that word in quotes because you and I both know you've done nasty stuff before, but *he* doesn't need to know that!) Start allowing him to unleash the sex goddess in you, even though you are merely recycling old moves . . . but, once again, he doesn't need to know that. Act shocked at how good it feels, and praise him for making you try something "new." Men do it all the time. For example, one of the oldest tricks guys use is convincing the new girl they're sleeping with that they've never tried anal sex and that they wanna try it with her for the first time. Meanwhile, a lot of guys have done it at least once before, but that's their ploy for getting a girl to do it with them. I know, they're bad sometimes, but we should be too.

TIP #25

Don't Admit You've Cheated

Honesty is, hands down, the best policy. Unless you've cheated. Then you should learn to embrace the half-truth.

Let's say that you're a good girl but a couple of relationships ago you made the mistake of cheating. It broke his heart and ruined your relationship, and you paid for it several times over. Two years and ten pounds later you finally got over it and forgave yourself. Now you're in a new relationship and the topic of cheating comes up. He asks if you've ever been unfaithful, and you have to make the call: Do I practice unbridled honesty and face the consequences, or do I keep my saintly image intact and shut it?

For heaven's sake, shut it, woman! Fib, lie, skirt the truth, call it what you must, so long as you don't tell him you've cheated. It may not sound like the most ethical solution, but I assure you it's the most practical. Why? Well, despite how much you think he'll appreciate your honesty, your cheating will make a bigger impression and seriously damage your image, credibility, and long-term girlfriend potential.

Think about it from a guy's perspective: You just found out that your girlfriend has had a problem with cheating in the past. This is the same girl who goes out twice a week dancing and drinking, dressed smoking hot with her girls (absent you). Uh-oh. Now that you know about her little moral deficiency, wouldn't your stomach do a flip or two every time she suited up for a night out? Sure, you trust her, but that little voice will keep reminding you of how hammered she gets when she goes out and how every guy is going to buy her drinks. Eventually you're going to lose your hair or your sanity, or most likely both.

The problem with men is they are more visual than women.

MAN: I hungry, I see burger, I want hamburger.
WOMAN: I hungry, I see burger, I wonder if it's a turkey burger?

When men hear you've cheated, it gets stuck in the back of their heads in a little crazy-jealous storage bin. The fuller it gets, the more awful your relationship becomes.

The thing is that most guys will jump ship long before the balding begins. If you're a chronic cheater you deserve to get the boot, but if you're a good girl who made a mistake five years ago, you don't. The solution is to keep your guy oblivious to your little slipup. You've heard the clichés: What you don't know won't hurt you. Out of sight, out of mind. No harm, no foul. Pick your favorite and stick to your story. Cheating: never have, never will.

Don't brand yourself with the scarlet letter and give your relationship a short shelf life. Just keep the cheating to yourself.

TIP #26

Don't Leave Sappy Notes

**Notes, much like sex with the lights on,
should only be reserved for special occasions.**

Unexpected notes are a great way to surprise someone and brighten his day. They're an even better way to demand ransom or threaten a life. The line between sweet and psycho is very thin, and I believe that the majority of note writers are totally oblivious to which side they're on. Not sure where you stand? Well here's a quick test to find out.

When writing your guy a note, have you ever . . .

1. Started the note with a pet name?
2. Described the way he looks when he sleeps?
3. Mentioned what the perfect car is for the eight kids you can't wait to have?
4. Signed your name in your own blood?

If you answered yes to any of these questions you're definitely a bad note writer, and good odds say that you've prematurely ruined a relationship or two. "But, Giuliana," you may be asking yourself, "aside from the Angelina Jolie–esque blood fetish, what's so wrong with this behavior?" To which I would lower my head in shame and cry a tear of sorrow for the future—and then I would proceed to tell you this.

1. Don't ever address your guy by his pet name in a note. It's bad enough that he has to tolerate the name calling while he's with you. Don't make him suffer while enjoying his private time. Also, should one of his friends find the note and discover that he goes by the name "Sweety-peety," he will surely suffer an unimaginable amount of ridicule that will someday force him into therapy.

2. For those of you who have had the rare misfortune of waking up to someone watching you sleep, I don't need to tell you just how creepy it is. Watching someone sleep isn't romantic, it's weird. If you're going to write something along the lines of, "You look just like a baby when you sleep," you might as well say, "I was watching you while you slept last night. P.S. I'm psycho."

3. Do I really need to beat this drum again? The guy you're dating doesn't want to know how he fits into your future family plans. This is especially true when you're planning on raising a small army. As a good rule of thumb you shouldn't be seriously discussing kids within the first six months of a relationship. And you definitely shouldn't bring up the topic in a note.

4. So you've tried signing your name in blood and it didn't work out the way you were hoping? Bummer.

How could that be? Oh, wait, I got it! The guy you're dating isn't from the planet Psycho like you. How could he understand such a thoughtful gesture? He's from Earth and lives in "reality" with the other six billion people who express their feelings normally. Adapt to the way we sane folk do things or prepare for a life of solitude.

TIP #27

Be a Good Cook or a Great Faker

Can't cook? Get the number of someone who can.

We've all heard the expression "The quickest way to a guy's heart is through his stomach," and as mature, adult women we all know that's complete bullshit. Come on, we're talking about guys here—the quickest way to their heart is right through the zipper. However, seeing as how we're self-respecting women we opt for the less whorish approach to getting the guy, hence the stomach expression. So food becomes our ally in the quest for landing a winner. And regardless of your experience in the kitchen you should not let your cooking skills, or lack thereof, be the cause of your relationship going sour.

There are only two types of women when it comes to cooking: those who grew up eating and those who grew up cooking. If you fall into the cook category, bravo. You've had plenty of practice in this arena and shouldn't struggle when it comes time to whip up some impressive cuisine. And I speak for all of the women who can't cook when I say, "Go eat a shit soufflé with a side of screw-you sauce," because you make us look bad with all of your warm cookies, pies, and cheese platters. If it weren't for all of you I would get away with serving a guy mac-and-cheese and pretzels for dinner, but no, you had to ruin it for the rest of us by raising the bar so high.

Clearly I'm not the most gifted in the kitchen, so there's a soft spot in my heart for you girls who think all food can and should be cooked in a microwave. Fear not, my cooking-impaired friends, for I have a quick fix: Fake it. Hold on, sister, I don't mean buy all the ingredients and pretend like you're cooking them and then hope it turns out right. No, that's a surefire way to a date ending in explosive diarrhea and severe food poisoning.

What I'm referring to is executing a "Fake-a-Bake," creating the illusion of having cooked by buying food that is already prepared. For example, tell your date to come over at seven-thirty, and at seven go pick up some impressive three-course meal from a restaurant you know is great. When he comes in, have the appetizer waiting on the table, the main course keeping warm in the oven, and the dessert waiting in the fridge. Of course you have to destroy all evidence that would incriminate you (i.e., boxes, bags, receipts). Next, put all the food on your own plates and even dirty up a couple of random pots and pans to leave in the sink so as to create the illusion of having cooked. He'll be quite impressed that you're capable of outcooking his mom. If he asks if you really cooked everything, have some fun with him. Say something like, "Well, Belvedere helped with the cocktails."

So you weren't born to wear a Kiss the Cook apron, no worries. Just remember, when it comes time to have him over for dinner have a couple restaurants on speed dial. It's the next best thing to being able to cook and beats the embarrassment of serving ramen and pizza rolls over candlelight.

TIP #28

Love Good Music

■

Marvin Gaye, good.
Ultimate Love Jams, **volume 8, bad.**

I realize that hiding your cheesy CDs may sound like a bit much, but you have to remember that guys, despite being universally inferior to women, are very perceptive. Don't let that vacant, glazed-over look on his face fool you: He notices when you play Chris de Burgh's "Lady in Red" three times during a thirty-minute car ride. It may not seem like a big deal to you, but for your guy to find *Ultimate Love Jams,* volumes 1–8, in your glove box would be like you finding a dead hooker in his trunk. It's bad. Very, very bad.

To you it's just a love song. It's something you listen to when you want to escape to that fantasy world where men still write love letters, cry, and profess their love to a woman about to get married in front of a crowded church (thank you, Michael Bolton). To guys, love music is a red flag. No, it's bigger than a flag. It's a gigantic red sail on the USS *Hopelessly Romantic.* Let him find your collection of tearjerkers and he will jump ship faster than you can say *Titanic*.

I'm not saying you can't have CDs packed with sappy love songs. Because you should. Love songs are good, and we need them. They make us smile when we are thinking of a new love and help us cry endlessly when we've been dumped. But as I said, guys don't view romantic music as such a positive thing, so that means you have one option: Stash it.

That's right, make like a pirate and bury that junk somewhere safe. Find a little spot where you're sure he won't look, like behind your stack of *Vogue* magazines or next to the box of tampons, and leave them there. Do not, and this bears repeating, *do not* leave your mushy music in your glove box. I realize that the little keyhole creates the illusion of security, but who really locks it? No one.

You should think of your collection of love jams like a guy's collection of porn: People assume that you have some but you never admit to it, and you certainly never let anyone find it.

TIP #29

Hide Your
Astrology Books

■

If you think his reaction to finding your stash of
Ultimate Love Jams is bad, just wait until he
uncovers Linda Goodman's *Sun Signs*.

TIP #30

Wax

■

**Sure, it's painful and expensive, but
so is a shiatsu massage and that hasn't
stopped you before, has it?**

Yes, I'm actually dedicating a whole entire tip to the act of waxing. Why? Because it is crucial that women keep themselves
well groomed if they're hoping to keep a guy biting at the bit.
Well, not biting—more like gently nibbling. Whatever, it's a
figure of speech. But let me make this point: It's not mandatory
that you wax. If you prefer, you can tweeze, thread, shave, trim,
laser, Nair, or do whatever else you want so long as you keep
yourself in tip-top shape. Maybe I should have titled this tip
"Wax, Tweeze, Thread, Shave, Trim, Laser, or Nair," but if
you've read the tip on brevity, you know that's not my style.

I think it's safe to say that the vast majority of women have, at
one time or another, experienced the unparalleled joy that is waxing. For those of you who have yet to wax, let me tell you that
you're missing out on a tremendous experience. And by tremendous I mean tremendously painful and humbling. Seriously,

every time I have a date with my waxer, I beg and plead for an epidural, but apparently there are legal issues and something about numbing myself from the waist down every two weeks that isn't "safe." Whatever. Apparently I just haven't found the right salon. Though truth be told, if waxing is any indication of how painful childbirth is, I'm adopting.

The only upside to waxing is that it's quick and will take your mind off all the other pain in your body. Oh, and there's one more benefit, the reason that we routinely subject ourselves to such barbaric torture: Guys love it. It's the smooth, bare, naked truth—guys appreciate good grooming. And after all the effort we put into our appearance—hair, makeup, nails, clothes, underwear—it just makes sense that we would keep up with the personal grooming. Why work so hard to look amazingly sexy only to blow it because were afraid of the wax job? That's like buying a top-of-the-line Mercedes and keeping the floor mats from your '83 VW Bug.

If waxing isn't your thing, then employ one of the other methods listed above—just do something. You don't need to be, or think, like a guy to appreciate good personal grooming. So take two Advils and make an appointment with your local waxer. But first be sure to ask if they give epidurals.

TIP #31

Don't Wear
Granny Panties

Unless you're dating the elderly, there is no
excuse for wearing granny panties.

Granny panties. The name alone should tell you something:
They're designed for women who have lost the fight against gravity and aging. Or they're marketed to women who are dating in
the "sixty to one hundred" age group. Either way, the purpose of
the granny panty is not to accentuate or show off the buttocks.
No, their sole function is containment—keeping the butt re-
gion from being further victimized by gravity. Much like a bib
for children, granny panties are worn as a preventive measure
rather than a fashion statement.

Underwear is a very personal thing, and as such it should not
be taken lightly. Your underwear is your calling card. It speaks
volumes about the type of person you are, and guys will look to
it as an indicator of how sexual you are. A small glimpse of a
sexy thong and he'll start thinking that you're a little vixen. But
he won't be able to find out without a date first, right? You

score: All it took was a small glimpse of the thong and he's relentlessly pursuing your number. However, the opposite is just
as true. Let a guy sneak a quick peek at your granny panties and
watch how quickly he loses interest. Here's how a guy's mind
works:

GRANNY PANTIES = BORING

GRANNY PANTIES + GIRL = BORING GIRL

BORING GIRL + NAKED TIME = ROBOTIC, MISSIONARY SEX

GIRL + GRANNY PANTIES = LOTS OF FREE WEEKEND NIGHTS

In just a matter of seconds he has already made up his mind
that you're not kinky or exciting simply based on the fact that
you choose to wear your mother's mother's underwear. What a
shame.

On the flip side, don't go over the top with the sexy underwear. As much as a guy likes seeing something sexy, too little
can be too much. Case in point: the dental-floss G-string that
you normally see only on the beaches of Brazil. This kind of underwear doesn't just grab attention; it also screams *hoochie* in six
different languages, including Portuguese. Yeah, not exactly the
foundation of a respectable outfit. Unless you're chasing frat
boys, you run the risk of a guy seeing your very slutty G-string
and immediately asking himself, "Nice underwear. I wonder
where she dances?" Congratulations, you're never going to meet
his parents.

TIP #32

Never Admit You've Had Plastic Surgery

Unless he was in the operating room with you, he can't ever really prove it.

Men don't know the difference. They really don't. When he calls you out on your boob job, respond like you are borderline offended and say, "What boob job?" When he gives you the "You must be joking" look—because clearly your boobs are harder than a physics test and besides, the little scars are a dead giveaway—just stick to your guns (no pun intended) and deny it. Tell him he's not the first person to accuse you of having implants and your boobs really are just that great.

As for your collagen lips or botoxed forehead, those are easy! Unless he storms into the doctor's office while you're getting the injections, there is no way he can prove it.

Bottom line: Let him think you are perfect for as long as possible.

TIP #33

Don't Be a Bad Drunk

■

Put down the Long Island iced tea and act like an adult. You're not in college anymore.

Alcohol is a wonderful thing. It makes crappy parties fun and ugly guys hot, and boosts the self-confidence like nothing else. On the flip side, it makes ugly guys hot, causes us to throw up, and makes us call our exes at two in the morning to explain how much we're over them. Trust me, no matter how hot you are, no guy is going to want you after he holds your bangs while you barf. Here's a conversation you'll never hear in a bar:

GUY: That's a really nice top you're wearing. Is that a little splash of puke on the sleeve? That's hot.

GIRL: My puke was green. (*looks around*) Where's my ride?

GUY: You puked? That's awesome, self-control and moderation are so overrated.

GIRL: Why did my ex break up with me? (*begins sobbing*)
   I'm so ugly.
GUY: Your personality rocks. Can I take you out some-
   time?

Guys like it when we drink so long as it leads to rowdy behavior, flirtation, and possibly sex—basically, when drinking causes us to start acting like we're in a beer commercial. They don't like it when it unleashes the hyperemotional, violent, marathon puker who requires constant attention.

Avoid becoming a burden by knowing—and respecting—your limits. Pretend like you're a lady and start sipping, not gulping, your drinks. Take the opportunity to show off your appreciation for a good drink and enjoy it slowly. Not only will he respect the fact that you know your booze, but it will help you temper the speed at which you get shit-faced. Excuse me, that wasn't very ladylike. I meant shit-canned.

TIP #34

Don't Nag Him to Validate Your Relationship

■

Be realistic: If you're looking for constant love and affection, you need a dog, not a boyfriend.

"Does this bikini make me look fat? Are you even paying attention to me? Do you still love me as much as you did since the last time I asked you six minutes ago? Do you think I'm insecure?"

I pity men.

Come on, ladies! We have made such progress in strengthening the image of the woman over the past fifty years—why do we let ourselves stoop to such a level? It's not like we learn it from watching the guys we date. How many times has a guy asked you, "Does this shirt make my triceps look small?" "If I gained thirty pounds would you still love me?" It is unfair to put your guy through this sort of twisted mind fuck. We even go so far as to ask questions that don't have a right answer. Does "Do you think she's pretty?" ring a bell?

Why women do this to men I don't understand, but the bottom line is, they shouldn't. It's not fair and will most certainly end a good relationship. Don't set unrealistic expectations on how your guy is going to express himself. A guy will show that he cares for you by spending time with you. If your guy skips a Friday night out with his friends to come over and watch a movie with you, he's showing you he cares. Once he gets there, don't ask him if he's really likes you. He's there—he likes you.

Guys also show affection by putting up with you. We're women, so by nature we spend one week every month being moody, short-tempered, and needy. This means that guys spend two weeks a month dealing with us. That's right: two weeks. Four days before (stocking up on chocolate and Midol, accepting the fact that he's about to go a whole week without great sex, dreading the verbal attacks), the actual week of, and three days after (apologizing to all of his friends for your behavior, making sure he's back on your "good" side). That's an awful lot of work—acknowledge it.

You should also avoid talking about how amaaazzzing your best friend's relationship is. How her boyfriend is so affectionate and understanding and devoted. How he's soooooo in love with her that he tells her he wants to be with her for the rest of his life and that one day, he's going to marry her and have tons of kids with her and travel all around the world together. Guys hate hearing that! All they hear is, "Why won't *you* marry me?!!" Instead, don't bring up your friend's relationship at all. And when the four of you go out to dinner and your friend and her guy are lovey-dovey and all over each other, act cool. When you part for the night, either don't mention it at all or, better yet, make fun of them! You and your guy will have a few good laughs and he'll think you are the best. Unlike his ex-girlfriend who gave him the cold shoulder all night the last time he took her out with his insanely affectionate coworker. Inside, you may be bubbling with envy, but on the outside, act as cool as a cucumber. Don't ask him why he's not more like your best friend's boyfriend.

When you consistently quiz your guy on his feelings for you and the status of the relationship, you do two things: First, you annoy him, and second, you remind him that you're insecure and needy, much like a child. So separate yourself from the six-year-olds and act like the self-confident woman he's more attracted to.

TIP #35

Try Not to Cry in Front of Him

Barring legitimately sad occasions—and no, the end of *The Notebook* doesn't count—you shouldn't let him catch you crying.

I know, I know, you're thinking, "Giuliana, crying is a natural, healthy emotional response. My boyfriend and I cry in front of each other all the time. What's so bad about it?" Wow, your boyfriend cries in front of you all the time? Well, congratulations, you've found your soulmate. You two were made for each other, like Dolce & Gabbana. As for the crying, I don't have anything against the act of crying itself. However, it becomes a problem when you start doing it in front of a guy at inappropriate times.

There are occasions, like a funeral, when crying is appropriate. In fact, in this case it's good to cry in front of your guy because if you don't, he might suspect he's dating a robot. And unless he's a science fiction junkie, that won't go over too well.

My beef is with the women who cry about as often as they sneeze and cough. They cry during Kodak commercials, while looking at old photos, even at the movies during the previews. These excessive waterworks will drive a guy away immediately. Guys don't like to console, they don't know what to say, so they just spout out random clichés until we stop crying. It's an uncomfortable act they really don't enjoy doing, especially on a triweekly basis.

If you were a guy, would you want to date a girl who cried every time you did something thoughtful, romantic, rude, or inconsiderate? Imagine that you forget to call one night and it really hurt her feelings, so you buy her a card to apologize, and then she reads the sweet message and starts crying all over again.

Unless you find a guy who thinks runny mascara is hot, you better learn to curb the tears.

TIP #36

Learn to Accept Football

■

**To most men, football isn't a sport;
it's a religion.**

He's your guy, your pet project. In the couple of months that you've been dating you've managed to smooth out his rough edges to the extent that he actually resembles a stylish, well-behaved gentleman. That is, until Sunday rolls around.

Gone is the near metrosexual you've been training and in his place is a football-loving, pigskin junkie. The hip shirt from Hugo Boss is replaced by a shirt so tattered and stained it looks like the tablecloth from last year's Thanksgiving dinner. His perfectly faded boot-cut jeans are a thing of the past. Today he's sporting a pair of sweatpants he's had since junior high that leave him looking like he shops in the gay-pirate-capri-pants section at Wal-Mart. Sweet Jesus.

You beg him not to wear this ridiculous ensemble, but regardless of how much you beg, threaten, and plead, he won't budge. Even your most vicious threat—no sex—falls on deaf ears. How is this possible?

Well, poor soul, it's Sunday. That's guy talk for game day— their sabbath, if you will. It is on this day that he resides in his La-Z-Boy and offers himself to the gods of the game. No matter how many weekends you've observed his ritual, it still doesn't make sense to you. "Why the horrendous outfit?" you plead. For good luck, of course. That's right, despite all of the years of grueling training and steroid use, his team needs him and that extra little dose of good luck he brings when he wears his lucky shirt and gay-pirate-capri-pants combo. Even if he watches the game at home, three thousand miles away from the stadium, it still helps. The football gods see his tireless dedication and reward him and his team with a victory.

So how do you combat this mighty beast and reclaim your man? You don't. Not if you're smart, that is. Getting your guy to stop watching football is a pipe dream, an impossibility. He will drop you years before he considers giving up the game. "Then, Giuliana," you ask, "what am I supposed to do?" Well, first, you should stop talking aloud to yourself in the middle of a crowded bookstore. Then, you should learn to embrace the damned game. That's right, if you can't beat him (over the head with a lead pipe), you might as well join him.

Learn to like the game. Find some aspect of it that you enjoy, be it the uniforms or the touchdown dances. Something. Anything that will keep your attention and keep you next to him on the couch is a good thing. The benefits to this are twofold: One, you get more quality time with him. Two, you'll probably be the first girlfriend he's had who actually "enjoyed" football, a point that he will appreciate tremendously.

TIP #37

Don't Drag Him Out Shopping

Taking a guy shopping isn't fun— it's cruel and unusual punishment.

There isn't a sale big enough to justify dragging your guy to the mall with you. Why? He will hate you for it. From the second your eyes glaze over at the sight of Bloomingdale's doors all the way down to when he's relieved of his duties as your personal shopper, he will be utterly miserable. And if you think that some serious time in the sack is going to make everything all right, well, you're right. Come on, we're talking about guys here. For them sex is like TheraFlu—it cures everything. You lied to him about hanging out with your ex? No problem, take it to the bed. You pawned your engagement ring to cover your ex's gambling debts? Okay, that's bad. How ever will you fix things? If you guessed doubling naked time with a little dirty talk, you're right, clever girl! But I digress. The point is, *do not* force him to go shopping with you.

Shopping is a beautiful thing. It is escapism at its finest. We spend hours trying on expensive clothes surrounded by professional motivational speakers. "You look amazing. No, glorious. No, positively radiant. I can't believe how well that dress slims you down while pulling attention away from your peg leg. You look like Julia Roberts in her prime." I repeat, shopping is a beautiful thing—*for women.*

Men do not like being dragged around a store and asked, "What do you think of this?" four hundred times. You walk into Macy's and see unending racks of beauty. He walks in and sees countless racks of the same shirt in thousands of different color variations. The only potentially enjoyable part of the experience is watching you change, but he's forced to sit in that lone chair in front of the changing rooms reserved for unlucky husbands and whipped boyfriends.

So he sits alone, ashamed to be "that guy" all the other guys pity, only to have you come out and interrogate him. "Does this top make me look fat? Really? Not even just a little? What about my butt, do you think it looks big? You do!? I can't believe you." (*begins sobbing*) "Why do you even come if all you're going to do is insult me?"

No wonder he cries every time a Macy's commercial comes on.

TIP #38

Don't Wear a Costume That Requires a Mustache

■

TIP #39

Don't Be a
Suck-Ass Driver

**Taking him on a date should feel like a
romantic car ride, not the opening scene
in *The Dukes of Hazzard*.**

Sure, it may seem a little nitpicky to focus on good driving, but
you have to realize that bad driving can bring a relationship to a
screeching halt, much like bad yellow-light etiquette.

I have friends who take bad driving to a whole new level.
They make left-hand turns from the right lane, they ride everyone's ass like a frat boy at a dance party, and their brakes take
more of a beating than Ben Affleck's career post-*Gigli.* It's as if
burning rubber is the smell they ask for when they get their cars
cleaned. "New-car freshener? Um, no. Do you have Burnt Rubber? Yeah, I really want it to smell like I drove down a mountain
with my emergency brake on." And yet when I ask them why
they don't do something to improve their horrendous driving,
they usually give an answer along the lines of, "I'm not a bad
driver. I'm just aggressive. Anyway, people love driving with
me. It's thrilling."

Here's the deal: The Jurassic Park water ride at Universal Studios is thrilling. Bad driving is scary. Jurassic Park doesn't risk your life. You may get squirted with water, but at no point are you at risk of being maimed or disfigured. Bad driving can cost you thousands in tickets and fines, injure others, and—listen up, you aesthetically gifted women—permanently ruin your hair and face. Don't jeopardize your bank account, great looks, and relationship by being a spaz behind the wheel.

If you already abide by the rules of the road, then read no further; this tip doesn't apply to you. But for you ladies who drive like Mario Andretti, we need to have a little heart-to-heart: If you drive like crap, the only thing he's going to be touching all night is the "Oh, shit!" bar (located above the passenger side window). Face it, Miss No Blinker Lane Change, you have a problem and it needs to be addressed.

As far as I'm concerned, you have two options: One, challenge yourself with one of the classes designed for sixteen-year-olds and learn the rules of the road. If that's too embarrassing, sign up for an online course or get a book. Now remember, after you learn the road rules, follow them. If the idea of spending four consecutive Saturdays with a group of hyperactive teenagers or reading a driving manual when you could be reading *Vogue* doesn't sound awesome, you can always opt for the easy alternative and never drive on dates. Yes, it is a little selfish, but so is letting him pick up the check every time, which we're about to get to next. Also, let us not forget that it beats the alternative— your next date ending with him taking the bus home. So don't think of it as a selfish move; think of it as a selfless gesture: You're saving him $1.50 in bus fare.

TIP #40

Don't Always Leave Him with the Bill

**Give your guy and his wallet a break every once
in a while and pick up the check.**

■

Have you ever noticed that most women on dates display the same post-meal, pre-check behavior? It's like clockwork: The plates are cleared, drinks are finished, and as the waiter in the background approaches, Miss Manners excuses herself and makes a beeline to the loo. After a couple of minutes, she returns to find that her date has paid the bill. Again. Like he does every time. Wow, what a sweetheart.

Knock it off, will ya?

You and I both know that you don't sprint to the bathroom because your bladder is beckoning. You do it to avoid the monetary kick in the pants more commonly referred to as The Bill. And why? Surely you aren't flat broke, because that Louis Vuitton bag didn't grow on a sale rack. Neither did those Gucci shades. Or the D&G top. Or even the Jimmy Choo shoes. Please, you're not broke by any means. The total cost of one of your outfits is more than the GDP of several small island countries put together. What's up now, Guam?

I think old-fashioned custom is primarily to blame for our dodgy behavior. Forty years ago it was appropriate to let the guy consistently pick up the check. But we're not living in the sixties, are we? Women have gained a significant amount of independence since then, and one of the ways we show it is through earning and spending our own money. And what better way to display your independence than through a selfless gesture like picking up the check? Sure, you could talk his ear off about the women's rights movement, but wouldn't it be a whole lot easier just to toss a little green his way?

Offer to pay for dinner once in a while and if he's the type of guy who won't let you grab the check, then every so often you should slip your credit card to the waitress on your way to the bathroom or when he's out of sight. When the check comes, he will always be pleasantly surprised. It's a classy move and he'll respect you for it.

TIP #41

Be Unconventional and Spontaneous

■

**Keep the relationship alive
by keeping him on his toes.**

Why do people love magicians? Sure, the flashy stretch pants make for a good laugh, but that's not it. Give up? Tah-dah! We love them because we never know what they're going to do next. It's exciting watching someone when you don't have a clue what they're dreaming up. One minute you're quietly sitting in your seat, and the next thing you know your watch is gone and your sister's pregnant. Ironically enough, women have something to learn from an industry entirely dominated by mysterious men; surprises and spontaneity are great ways to keep a guy's attention.

Most relationships start to fizzle out around the three-month mark, after what I refer to as the "honeymoon period." Unfortunately, most women make the mistake of letting the relationship start to drag before they try to bring it back to life. Don't let this happen. The key to keeping him interested is to be spontaneous and look for unconventional ways to spend time with him.

Let's say you and your guy have started doing dinner and a movie every week. At first it's nice—it requires no real planning or forethought, you get to eat good food, veg out, and eventually go back to your place for a little naked time. This is all fine and well until the tenth time you're doing it and it feels more like a tradition than a fun date. Remember this: If *you* feel like things might be getting a little dry, he's *definitely* bored. Guys have much shorter attention spans than women and if you're not constantly introducing new bells and whistles into the equation, he's going to get comfortable, get bored, and move on to the next girl.

Don't give him the opportunity to get tired of the relationship. Have unique date ideas: Plan a weekend getaway to wine country, go to a football game and have a tailgate party, try an extreme sport, take a quick one-night trip to Vegas. You can't go wrong so long as you think outside of the dinner-and-a-movie box. Your creativity will go over especially well if he's not very imaginative and used to run-of-the-mill dates. Not only will he like you thinking on your own, but he'll love the fact that you're introducing him to new things. As a result of your unconventional ideas, he'll come to associate you with the fun he has every time you go out. This means you won't have to worry about his losing interest in the relationship, seeing as how he's dating the epicenter of fun.

TIP #42

Don't Try to Break His Bad Habits

Guys are full of bad habits. Change only what you absolutely must. Save the relationship—and your sanity—by choosing your battles wisely.

Men may have better posture than their cousins, the apes. But they sure have a lot of bad habits in common.

Guys have been scratching themselves for thousands of years. What makes you think you'll be able to break the habit in a matter of months? It's just not possible. One, he'll tire of your incessant nagging and lose you like a kid at the mall. And two, *you'll* eventually go crazy from the sound of your own voice.

This may seem far-fetched, but I have a girlfriend who once told me she was getting tired of listening to herself scold her boyfriend for leaving dirty dishes all over the house. That's right, tired of listening to herself. Needless to say, that guy has since relocated to a different house with a new, significantly less anal-retentive girl.

If you're going to pick a cause to get behind, make it something noble, like eliminating poverty or finding a cure for stupidity (because clearly it's a genetic issue that plagues single women ages twenty-five to forty). Don't waste your time, or his, by attempting to change every little quirk that doesn't fit with your image of the perfect guy. Your perfect guy doesn't exist. And even if he did, he'd probably be gay, so let the dream die.

However, should the new guy you're dating be so overflowing with faults that you need to do some character remodeling, do it intelligently. Only pick habits that you're certain he'll be able to part with eventually. For example, getting him to stop wearing his baseball hat inside the house is realistic because it's a habit based on routine and he probably does it without thinking. However, *do not* try and stop him from anything that he does with his friends. It's bad enough your guy sees that you're trying to domesticate him, but as soon as his poker buddies find out, they'll be reminding him 24-7 what a tight-ass you are and how lame he's becoming. That's twenty-four times a hand, seven hands every thirty minutes. It's relationship disaster.

I realize this concept may not make sense to all the women reading this. Allow me to make an attempt at clarification through a fictional scenario. Let's say you hate it when your guy smells like he's been napping in a humidor, so you try to get him to stop smoking cigars during poker night with the guys. While this may sound fine to you, let's look at it from the guy's angle. You just put your man on trial for dating a cigar-hating Fascist. The jury? His poker buddies. The evidence? A slew of notes, voice mails, and emotional scarring all targeted at his poker-night stogie antics. After seconds of deliberation, the jury reaches a verdict and it's unanimous: He's been found guilty of three counts of dating his mother. The sentence? A long, happy life absent you, with the possibility of dating one of your cooler friends.

Don't try to tackle serious social habits like this until after the wedding, maybe even after the first child is born. Be smart—avoid trying to change habits that are going to require a significant amount of prodding. Remember, there are hordes of women out there who will tolerate his faults, and he knows it.

Think about it. Does your boyfriend ever nag you about the way you brush your teeth or the fact that you keep six different types of bubble bath on the tub? Does he scold you when you don't fold your clothes and put them away nicely? Does he huff and puff every time you leave your damp towel on the bed? No, he doesn't, and if you answered yes to three or more of those questions, he may be gay and you may want to move on.

The fact is, men don't let the small things bug them. As long as you're not making any major mistakes, they keep their cool. And so should we.

TIP #43

Don't Buy Him Clothes You Want Him to Like

The only type of clothing you should ever buy a guy is sexy lingerie. For you, not him. Unless, of course, he's a cross-dresser.

You can spot that poor guy a mile away: uncomfortable smile, awkward posture, eyes watering on the verge of crying, and an all-too-proud girlfriend beaming at the Kelly green sweater he's trapped in. She bought it for him and now he's forced to live in his own personal cashmere hell. His friends will gawk and laugh, and so will strangers, because clearly he's the victim of a heinous fashion crime—the gift from a girlfriend, otherwise known as the "Since you have no fashion sense I thought I would buy you something my gay friends wear even though you would normally never be caught dead in it" gift.

It's just not fair to do this to a guy. You know that he lives in jeans, sweats, and the same three T-shirts he's had since college. Why would you buy him a pink pin-striped dress shirt from Nordstrom? You know he won't like it, won't want to wear it, and will resent you for making him dress like a clown. He will wear it—but don't fool yourself into thinking it's because he turned metro overnight and suddenly likes it. No, he'll wear it because you are the gatekeeper to sex, and if he offends you he might as well put naked time in a box and send it away. So the shirt will go on and his pride will go out the window.

What you have to realize is that over time, these "gifts" (note the quotation marks) will take a toll on him, and on the relationship. Think about it. He spent the first ten to fifteen years of his life being dressed by his mother—do you think he wants to relive that trauma all over again with you? Metro shirts and pants so tight they threaten his future offspring are a one-way ticket to Friday-night threesomes between you, Ben, and Jerry.

I realize that the gift of clothes comes from a good place; all you want is to do something nice for him. What you have to realize is that buying clothes for a guy is a total cluster-fuck. First you spend time and money getting the sweater, then he has to wear it out and spend anywhere from three to seven miserable hours looking like your well-dressed gay friend, and the whole time he's thinking about his ex, who never made him dress like the sixth member of the *Queer Eye for the Straight Guy* team.

Look at what happens because of one bright cashmere sweater: You lose a couple of valuable shopping hours, a hundred bucks, and a boyfriend. He loses his pride, his dignity, and any respect his friends once had for him. No one wins when you buy him cashmere. Or silk. Or anything from a store that doesn't sell flip-flops or sports jerseys.

Be a smart girlfriend by being a selfish shopper: Buy clothes for yourself.

TIP #44

Avoid Celebrating Every Single Occasion

■

**Don't let Hallmark fool you;
you don't need a card for every occasion.**

Guys have a hard enough time remembering their own birthdays, what makes you think they're going to remember your X-month anniversary? Guys don't measure relationships in days, weeks, or even months—they only see years. This means that when you break out the "Happy One Month" anniversary card, you're bound for some awkward conversation: "Wow, is it our one-month anniversary already? It feels like it's only been, well—a month since we met. I guess in dog years that's a long time, right?"

Not every event is a milestone. Six weeks from the first time he slept over—without being drunk—is not noteworthy. Don't celebrate it. In fact, don't even mention it. The mere fact that you're keeping track of how long it's been will seriously weird him out.

Don't make him feel like a little kid by celebrating everything he does. I think many women believe that a guy will like them more if they constantly shower him with compliments. Excessive amounts of praise are reserved for puppies and babies, not grown men. Not only is it unnecessary, which will make you look insincere, but it will make him feel awkward and potentially insulted. If he changes the light bulb in the hallway and you launch into a ten-minute monologue about how amazing he is, you're going to lose serious points. He didn't solve cold fusion; he changed a light bulb. Pat him on the back and point him in the direction of the next repair.

Guys buy cards for two events: funerals and your birthday. This is because guys don't celebrate to nearly the extent that women do. For some guys it is due to sheer laziness, while others genuinely don't like making a big deal of things. Either way, you need to realize that getting your guy on board the card, candy, and flower train may be an uphill battle.

Don't ruin a special day by nagging him to give you a card with a heartfelt inscription. Just because you fill up the entire card with a declaration of your love doesn't mean that he has to. If you're expecting Shakespeare, you're in for some serious disappointment. Odds are you'll get something on a par with "Roses are red, violets are blue." Regardless of what he writes, so long as he tries, let him know that you appreciate the gesture. If you chastise him for not writing more or not being romantic enough, you're going to hurt his feelings and leave him dreading the next anniversary.

TIP #45

No Tattoos of Affection

■

**Find less permanent ways to
express your love, like promise rings or
sappy license plate frames.**

Even on its worst day, the barbed-wire armband tattoo is nowhere near as embarrassing as an ex's name permanently tattooed on your body. Having "Gus" in cursive on your ankle is like wearing a modern-day scarlet letter. You'll be forced to showcase your badge of embarrassment for the rest of your life and never stop answering the question, "Mommy, who's Gus? Is that Daddy's middle name?" Ouch.

Tattooing your current infatuation's name on your body isn't a small boo-boo. It's a catastrophic mistake measuring an 8.3 on the screw-up scale. Not to mention the fact that it's begging fate to curse your relationship. Can we say Angelina Jolie? Unless her pet name for Brad is Billy Bob I think she's wishing someone had pulled her aside a couple of years ago and talked her out of permanently inking Slingblade's name on her arm. Yes, I'll admit that she's pulled it off without much backlash, but let us not forget that she's Angelina Jolie. She's rich, famous, and arguably the most beautiful woman on the planet, and she's dating the only thing more amazing than that diamond from *Titanic*.

However, let's say you find yourself so utterly blitzed by your new guy that you feel compelled to perform a senseless act of devotion. A tattoo is your first choice, but seeing as how that is now out of the question, what options are you left with? How about a card? Or love letter? Or romantic date? Or surprise vacation? Or any alternative preferred by the sane population of adults? A tattoo is a brash, irreversible, immature show of affection. A guy's name tattooed on your shoulderblade is as romantic as a barbed-wire armband is tough. For shit's sake, Pam Anderson has a barbed-wire tattoo! In what imaginary world is she tough, aside from *Barb Wire,* that awful action film she starred in?

Here's the bottom line: You're not Angelina or Pam, you're a self-respecting, mature woman. The only guy's name that should ever be on your body is Giorgio Armani.

TIP #46

Don't Own a Dog
That Fits in Your Purse

TIP #47

Don't Drag Him to All Your Outings

It's bad enough that you have to put up with your coworkers. Don't make him suffer too.

Ah, the dreaded company Christmas party. And who can forget the painful company casino night. (Seriously, how can you have alcohol and gambling at a party and it still sucks?) And let's not leave out the nightmarish . . . you get the picture. Unless you work for a place that makes alcohol or shoots music videos, your company parties suck.

Most play out like this: You're trapped in some small area with all of the people you never invite to lunch, and it isn't until conversation dies ten minutes into the party that you realize why you eat alone. But wait, there's hope. The lady who's had too much to drink (every party has at least one of these) decides to save the conversation by pouring her heart out about her train-wreck marriage and how the food in rehab is much better than prison food. Meanwhile, the only thought racing through your head is, "Would it be rude to ask if I'm getting paid for this time?"

It makes sense that you would want to bring a guest to one of these parties. After all who's going to make sure the coast is clear while you're making a third trip to the dessert table? However, don't make the mistake of taking a boyfriend. For starters, by introducing him to your coworkers you're inviting them into your personal life. And one of the rules is that you never talk about your personal life with your coworkers. Why? Because the office is the epicenter of gossip. If you don't know any of your office's gossip it's probably because it's all about you. Don't give them anything to talk about, especially your love life.

Gossip aside, the main reason you never take a guy to your company functions is because these parties are awkward, uncomfortable, and emotionally taxing. It's one thing to drag him to the opera because it requires very little of him. He just sits and pretends to watch. It's an entirely different issue when he's forced to spend hours making small talk with the weird IT guy and consoling the crying woman whose name he doesn't even know (though after the party he'll be able to tell you all about her runaway daughter and how her therapist never listens). It's not fair to put him through this because at least you get paid to put up with them. He's doing it pro bono.

TIP #48

Make Him Feel Like You Don't Rely on Him

Don't let him think that he's the only one for you.

I don't care how comfortable you get with a guy. I don't care how long you've been dating. Heck, I don't care how long you've been engaged, or even married. A guy should never, ever feel like he has you completely. You should never give him the security of knowing that you can't live without him. That if he was to break up with you tomorrow, or even a year from now, you'd be devastated and want to kill yourself. It's OK to fall in love with a guy and let him know you are committed and love him to bits, but making him feel like a breakup would lead you to suicide—that's a whole other thing.

When you let a guy feel that there is no one else in the entire world you could be with, you are giving him too much power. You are giving him the power to walk away from you, or at least threaten to walk away from you. Even if he loves you to death and has no intention of leaving you, he still knows he has the power to dangle that in your face every time he wants something from you. Whether it's going to a football game, or Vegas with the boys, or even something as simple as wanting Italian instead of Chinese, when a guy knows he's gotcha, trust me, he's gotcha!

Don't give up the power of possession you have of yourself. One time, my boyfriend and I were having an argument over the craziest thing. It was about four or five months into the relationship and we were as close and in love as you can get in four or five months. He was driving me insane with accusations that I was hot for some guy I had met the year before. No matter how much I denied it, or how crazy I told him he was being, he wouldn't let it go. It was driving me up the wall. The argument started at dinner and continued to my place where I changed into my pj's and got into bed. All the while he was standing there flailing his arms in the air, yipping and yapping, the accusations flying. Finally, as he stood there bitching, I pulled up the covers and turned off the lights. Silence. I said, "You're wrong. I'm right. Now get into bed. Otherwise, leave. I'm going to sleep." Silence. After a few seconds he said, "Fine, then I'll leave. What are you gonna do then?" I sat up, turned on the light, and looked him right in the face with the most confident, nonchalant look I could muster, and said, "Nothing. Not a damn thing. My life was great before I met you, so I'll be just great. Bye." I turned off the light and pulled up the covers. Within thirty seconds, he crawled into bed like a wounded puppy.

The next morning, everything was perfect again. No mention of the night before. About six months later, we were at dinner with friends when the incident came up again. Someone asked him how we met and what made our relationship work so well. He went into our whole story from our very first date to the time we went to London and more. Then suddenly, to my total and utter shock, he said something I will never forget. He looked at me and looked around the table and said, "As for the secret to why I love her so much? One night in the middle of an argument, Giuliana looked at me and said something along the lines of 'My life was great before I met you,' and right then and there, I had an epiphany. I realized that I had someone really special, not some girl just dying for a boyfriend or dying to get married. I knew that she was with me for me and because of how I treated her. And that if today or tomorrow I royally screw up, she'll walk right out the door. Therefore, I will *never* screw up, trust me!" Pretty sweet, huh?

Oh, in case my ex is reading this, I was *never* hot for what's-his-name.

TIP #49

Don't Doodle Your First Name with His Last Name

TIP #50

Let Him Say
the L Word First

Let him be the first to initiate the
"marriage" and "kids" and "move in
together" conversations.

When a guy is ready to say "I love you," he will say "I love you."
When a guy is ready to ask you to move in to his place, he will
ask you to move into his place. When a guy is ready to get married,
he will ask you to get married. Easy, right? Not so much. Most
girls can't let things happen organically. They push and push and
push a guy into saying and doing what they want him to say and
do. And all this does is piss a guy off and chase him away.

Eventually, the topics of love, marriage, and kids will come
up. Try not to bring them up until he initiates those conversations. I realize most guys are major procrastinators and unless
you nudge them, they won't budge. But I said nudge, not push
or jab or threaten! I'm telling you, if you hold off on mentioning
anything about marriage, he will eventually bring it up in some
subtle way (that is, if he likes you enough to even consider marrying you one day). Your reaction will dictate if he ever brings it

up again. If you act too excited or start jumping up and down like an idiot, then chances are, he may never bring it up again. But if you act really cool and even politely dismiss his suggestion with a little shrug, before long he will be so impressed that he will bring it up again and again and again.

If you just act like it's not your priority, your guy will see to it that it becomes your priority.

TIP #51

Say What You Really Mean

■

No means no. Yes means yes.

When you ask a guy what he wants to do and he says, "I'm hungry. Let's go grab dinner," do you know what he's really trying to say? Give up? What he really means is he's hungry and wants to grab dinner. Women, on the other hand, say one thing but mean another. Picture this scenario. Your guy suggests you two go meet his buddy for dinner. He says, "Do you wanna go meet my friend for dinner tonight?" If you do, great! But if not, don't lie and say, "Yeah, sure," then proceed to be a royal bitch on the car ride to dinner. When he asks you why you're being so bitchy and you say, "I wish we had just gone to dinner alone tonight," then you have successfully ruined dinner for yourself, your guy, and his friend, who senses something is brewing between the two of you.

Put a smile on your face; otherwise, his friend is gonna tell him "She sucks" the next day. You should have told him exactly what you wanted to do. Either he would have had dinner with you, or he would have gone out with his friend and met you after. But now, you screwed up and that's one strike against you.

TIP #52

Don't Always Drop Everything for Him

You have your own life, right?

Picture this: You come home from a stressful day at work to find your man sitting in front of the TV watching football with a cold beer and a smile on his face. He notices you're stressed out and tells you to kick off your shoes, grab a glass of wine, and join him on the couch. You mosey on next to him just as a commercial break begins and he sweetly puts his arm around you and asks you to recount the awful fight you had with your boss. You start recounting the details of your terrible day when suddenly the game comes back on. What happens next is what constitutes the difference between men and women.

Even though you are in the midst of recounting your miserable story, he shushes you and tells you to hold off until the next commercial break. How rude, right? Well, all men do this. Men, by nature, have their mind set on watching that football game, and nothing is gonna get in their way, not your problems, not even their own problems. Women, on the other hand, will mute *Desperate Housewives* and give their man their undivided attention. So where does this leave us? Well, most women get annoyed and storm off. A fight brews, you ignore each other, and your day ends up even worse than before. Finally, you ask yourself, "Am I really going to break up with him over a football game?" To which you answer, "No." You kiss, make up, and fall asleep.

So the bottom line is this: If we can't beat men in the "Honey, can this wait until the commercial break" department, we might as well join them. Let's say he comes home from work stressed out one night and catches you in the middle of your favorite must-see sitcom. He kicks off his shoes and starts telling you all about his crummy day, assuming you are going to mute the television and listen to his every word. What you need to do is start listening and then suddenly cut him off as soon as something exciting happens on the screen. Say something like, "Just a second, honey, this is the best part." If he storms off, roll your eyes, sigh, apologize, and tell him to go on with his story. You're still going to end up getting all the details of his day, you can be compassionate and nurturing, you can accomplish all the things you wanted to as a woman—but at least now, he will respect and appreciate your time a little more. The more you do this, the more he will value your undivided attention. He'll realize how annoying it is when he needs to get something off his chest, and stop treating you that way. Eventually, he will even adjust his behavior and be more attentive to you when you need him to listen, even if he's watching a football game.

TIP #53

Let Him Go to Vegas— Yes, Let Him Go

Remember the last time you heard a sweet story come out of Vegas? You don't? That's because there aren't any! Letting your man go to Sin City with his friends could end up in sin if you approach it the wrong way.

Ah, Vegas. Gambling, alcohol, drugs, and hookers. All things you don't want your boyfriend to be exposed to. Especially all at once and all in one night. But as a cool girl, you must learn to accept the fact that at least once in your relationship, your man will utter the dreaded one-liner, "I'm going to Vegas with my friends." Ouch!

I know, I know. That statement cuts deeper than an old razor blade, but it's a harsh reality that women all over this great country must come to terms with, hopefully not more than once in a lifetime.

As you're reading this you are probably thinking—or praying—that I will instruct you to bust out with some amazing strategy to keep your man from going to Vegas and convince him to stay at home instead. Well, your prayers have come true!

Just kidding. The harsh reality is that you must let him go on that dreaded trip with his disgusting friends. Now you're probably shouting, "But wait, Giuliana, he's an IT wiz and his friends are really nice, clean-cut guys." I'm sure they are back in Springfield, Missouri, but in Vegas they're disgusting. They're going to go to the Crazy Horse, and they're going to lose all their money on blackjack at the Hard Rock. But you gotta let him go! He's not going to run off with a stripper, and if he does, good riddance. You're not going to wake up Monday morning and find out he's met the women of his dreams in Vegas and she hangs off a pole for a living. If that happens, then thank God you let him go and never had babies with him.

He has a better chance of hitting the million-dollar jackpot at the slots than finding a woman better than you in Vegas. Let him have a crazy night and wake up miserable and missing you. The cooler you are this time, the more he may not want to go next time.

TIP #54

Don't Fight in Public

Believe it or not, the entire grocery store doesn't want to listen to you fight. If they want drama, they'll pick up an issue of *Star* magazine.

Fights, when conducted in a civil, mature fashion, are healthy occurrences in a relationship. So long as both parties refrain from turning the situation into an Ike and Tina affair and look to find some understanding, there's no problem. However, there are those who choose not to abide by the tips and make fighting a useless exercise in kicking and screaming.

Take, for example, the men and women who absolutely love the sound of their own voices. These precious gems will often pick fights just to listen to themselves scream. There is no point to the fight, and, accordingly, there is no solution. This means that the fight carries on until the unsuspecting victim has broken down or broken up with the shouter. For those of you who fall into this category, do yourself the favor of buying a tape recorder and taping your next fight. Not only will you realize what a complete spaz you are upon listening to it, but the next time you want to listen to yourself scream, you can listen to the tape instead of ruining another relationship.

Let us now turn our attention to the most atrocious form of fighting—the public fight. That's right, on the list of "shameful forms of fighting," public fighting is up there on top, right above cock fighting. Why? It's embarrassing for the people fighting and it's uncomfortable and annoying for the bystanders within earshot.

It's bad enough that people see your lack of self-control, but when you start the mudslinging you really lose face. For starters you're going to embarrass the hell out of your guy, which is a serious no-no. (He probably doesn't want all of aisle 3 knowing he "took" your virginity.) You'll make him mad for treating him like a child and make him look bad for dating such a raging psycho. And don't forget that in the process of making him feel like a jerk you're going to come off like the Mayor of Bitchville to everyone who witnesses your tirade.

Solution: If you're going to take off the gloves and start swinging, do it at home where no one sees. This way when you break up and he starts telling people that you're psycho, there won't be hordes of supermarket shoppers willing to back up his story.

TIP #55

Keep Your Family Out of Your Fights

∎

**Your dad already owns a shotgun and shovel.
Don't give him a reason to use them.**

It's hard not to bitch to your family about the drama in your life. After all, you've been doing it for the past twenty-some years and that's what family is for, free therapy. However, there is one area of your life that you cannot share with your family, and that is man drama. No matter how great the temptation to vent to your family about your relationship, you must resist or it will haunt you until the day you die. Or break up, whichever comes first.

Surely you've already brought a couple of duds home, so your parents have good reason to be wary of your new guy. Don't give them any reason to dislike him—they'll find plenty on their own.

Let's say that you just got into a fight with your new guy, so you call your mom to vent. You tell her what an insensitive jerk he is, and really lay on the dramatics to get her to side with you, which she does. You finish venting, she consoles you, and an hour later your relationship is as good as new. Everything's great and back to normal, right? Wrong, because she's going to turn around and tell your dad and brother what an asshole that new guy is and how he made you cry. Seeing as how neither of them have met Mr. New, all they know of him is that he's a prick and he makes you cry. Wow, this one's off to a great start.

Now, no matter how good he is, your family is always going to remember him as the jerk. Even if he's a superstar boyfriend for the next two years, you'll still be reminded of "that time he made you cry." And every time he visits, he'll be reminded, too. Your dad will give him the death-grip handshake and respond to him in two-word sentences. Your mom won't take down the old pictures of you and your ex, and your gay brother won't even hit on him; even the family poodle won't hump his leg. And when he finally picks up on the fact that he's not welcome, he'll ask you why. You'd better lie like a bastard, because admitting that you tell your parents about every fight will not go over well.

So perhaps what I said about family providing free therapy wasn't entirely true. Sure, they don't actually charge you to vent, but after the hundredth time that you hear "I told you so" or "Remember that time when he . . . ," you may want to take to the bottle, which will easily cost you hundreds of dollars.

Save yourself the time and money by saving the man drama for your friends, not your family.

TIP #56

Don't Let Yourself Go

Note to self: Five weeks into a relationship is not the time to start throwing away your makeup and sexy underwear.

During the first few months of your new relationship, you are the very essence of perfection in your guy's eyes. Everything you say and do is cute, and he'll think you're hot in everything you wear. It's great. His expectations are easy to exceed and it seems like you can do no wrong.

Then you hit the twelve-week mark and suddenly the fun train derails. All of your little quirks that were once so charming have lost their appeal (how can snorting when you laugh be anything but sexy?) and you have to try much harder to keep his attention. He even stops laughing at your jokes ("What do gay horses eat?") even though you've only told them to him thirty-six times. By the way, gay horses eat "haaaaay." (You have to say it in a really effeminate way to get the full effect.)

The best way to prepare for the shell shock of the twelve-week mark is to not let yourself get too comfortable in the relationship.

The day you stop trying to impress him is the day he starts wondering what he did with that other girl's number. Don't ever stop being the hot, mysterious girl you were the night you met him. That's right, keep the granny panties in the back of the drawer where they belong and don't be a stranger to your makeup cabinet. When the two of you are on a date he should feel like he's lucky to be out with you, not like he's doing some frumpy girl a favor.

I realize this can be quite difficult once the relationship progresses and you start spending much more time together. It's hard looking your best when you're sleeping over at each other's houses. Just be realistic and keep yourself in check. It's inevitable that he sees you without your makeup in the morning. But he doesn't need to be seeing you like that at five-thirty in the evening when he comes over after work . . . four days a week. He's clean and well-groomed, so why should you be dressed like a thrift-store mannequin? You shouldn't.

TIP #57

Stop Comparing Him to Your Ex

■

Guys never compare their current girlfriend to their ex—at least not to her face.

Ugh! Do I even have to write more than one sentence about this one??? Yes. Yes, I do. It seems like such an obvious one, yet it's a mistake women make over and over again. They talk about their ex to their new guy, and not only do they talk about him but they actually have the audacity to compare new guy to the ex-boyfriend. Cute, caring, sensitive ex-boyfriend. The one with the father who loooooved you and the mother who adored you so much, she gave you one of her mother's bracelets for your birthday. The ex who you would have probably married had you two been just a few years older when you dated. The one who has the amazing job and just bought a new house in the suburbs three months ago.

Yuck! Makes me sick! Worse, makes your new guy sick. Why are you subjecting him to these stories, huh? What good is it gonna do to burn the image of your ex-almost-husband into new guy's memory? Why put him through this torture when you can just kick him in the nuts and call it a night? Chances are, he'll find the nuts thing more tolerable than the "I'm nuts for my ex" thing. Save the reminiscing for your girlfriends.

Stop talking about the ex—*ex*cept to your best friends.

TIP #58

Be a Good
Travel Companion

Pack light, embrace the unexpected,
and no matter how bad things get,
try and laugh at the situation.

You're looking at your four bags packed to the brim and you're
going through a mental checklist of everything you need: Fourteen different tops? Check. Ten pairs of pants? Check. Eight
pairs of shoes? Check. Thirty-six pounds of makeup and accessories? Check. One frustrated, soon-to-be-burdened-like-a-mule
boyfriend? Check. Great! Looks like you have everything you
need for the perfect weekend getaway.

The first and most important tip for being a good travel companion is packing light. I realize this can be a difficult task for
hard-core accessorizers and fashion fiends, but you need to realize
how much guys hate dealing with your ten bags (not counting
your dog's luggage). Overpacking tells a guy three things: You're
high-maintenance. His back is going to be sore. And roughing it
is out of the question. Unless one of those bags contains a tent
and some ponchos, he's going to think you're not the camping

type. Remember, guys want a girl who can enjoy the ground underneath a tree as well as the suite at the Four Seasons. Show him that you're capable of doing both by not overpacking.

Another major component of good travel etiquette is being flexible and embracing the unexpected. Rarely does everything on a trip go according to plan, so it is crucial that you can handle the occasional mishap. Arriving in Rome and finding out that your luggage is on its way to Barcelona? Yeah, it's a burn, but berating him in the middle of a crowded airport isn't going to get your bags to you any sooner. And remember that it could be worse; you could have arrived in Rome pregnant with a stuttering problem, so just be thankful that's not the case.

I think a smart move is to use the catastrophe as an excuse to buy a new outfit or two and some lingerie. Think about how he is going to see it: You turned a crappy setback into an awesome experience (shopping spree for you, extra sexy naked time for him). No doubt your stock will go through the roof for that one.

Perhaps the most important quality of a good travel companion is being able to laugh it off. When things start to go wrong, who would you rather be stuck next to in a crowded bus? Mr. Poopy Pants who is bent on spending the day frowning and complaining about his bad luck, or the guy who says to hell with it and tries to make the best of the situation? It's a no-brainer; no one likes a sourpuss. Do your best to keep morale high and the trip fun by having a sense of humor.

Be a rock star travel buddy: Pack only what you're going to carry, plan on not having a plan, and when the shit hits the fan, laugh.

TIP #59

Forget Stuff

■

"Oh my gosh! It totally slipped my mind."

Do remember his birthday and your anniversary. *Don't* remember the exact time you first had sex or how long it lasted.

Before I dive into this issue let me clarify one point: When I use the word "forget" I mean two things: One, completely forget the event so that it's not lingering in the back of your mind, and two, if you can't forget the event, just don't bring it up. If you don't mention it, as far as he knows, you don't remember it. There you have it, either forget stuff or just don't bring it up. Now on to the filler.

I do not advocate being absentminded and forgetting important events like birthdays and special occassions. Surely if you don't remember his birthday you won't be around to forget the next one. No, that kind of forgetfulness is rude, inconsiderate, and a surefire approach to keeping yourself single.

My beef is with you girls who remember the most obscure

events, dates, and times and then remind your guy of them like they're a bona fide occasion. For example, a couple is lying in bed and suddenly the girl shrieks, "Oh, my God! Do you know what time it is?" Immediately the guy springs into panic mode, "Is it her birthday? Our anniversary? Is she late?"

The girl picks up the alarm clock, "Look, it's 1:34 A.M. That was the time on the clock when we started making love for the first time. I remember because if you mix the numbers up you get 143, which is pager code for 'I love you.' And then at 1:37 A.M you went to sleep. I remember because 1 minute and 37 seconds is almost exactly half as long as the sex lasted." Insert dumbfounded boyfriend here.

There are two big reasons why you shouldn't remember obscure events and times: First, you look like a psycho. When you remember the most random minutia of your relationship, you give the impression that he is the most important thing in your life. You don't want him to think he's on the top of your attention totem pole. No, keep him somewhere in the middle, and he'll keep trying to climb to the top. If he gets the impression that you think about him all day long, he'll recognize that the chase is over and get bored.

The second reason you should avoid remembering and bringing up weird events is that you put him in an awkward position. How is he supposed to respond to the 1:34 A.M. comment? "Oh, awesome! How about a hug?" You make him uncomfortable and he's not going to want to hang out with you if you're constantly quizzing him on "What happened on that bench?" and "What does that smell remind you of?"

Trust me, if you start forgetting dates more often and rehashing special events less often, he will think you are so cool. In fact, he will start remembering special occasions and moments that he normally would never talk about. And think how awesome you'll look when Mr. Right says, "Don't you remember, today is our six-month mark? How could you forget that?" Only to have you scrunch your forehead and say, "Is it? Oh, yeah, it is! I'm so sorry, I must've forgotten. I've just been so crazy with work that it completely slipped my mind."

So remember: Forget stuff.

Alex, age thirty-one, Chicago

I dated this girl in college who felt compelled to celebrate every little occasion and anniversary we had. We dated for about six and a half months and we must have had three "major" anniversaries and at least five "minor" ones. (Reality check: They were all pretty minor.) The "major" anniversaries were the one-month anniversary, the three-month anniversary, and the six-month anniversary (which fell about a week before Valentine's Day). The minor anniversaries were the one-month anniversary of our first kiss, the one-week anniversary of the first time we slept together, the one-month anniversary after we slept together. I know there were more, but I've mentally blocked them out to preserve my sanity. There were also countless other reminders of her flawless romantic memory: "Oh my God, this is the first place we ever held hands!" "That was the first movie we ever saw together!" And my favorite, "Aaawww, you're getting pancakes? That was what you ordered the first time we went out to breakfast!"

I really wish I was just being creative and funny, but I'm not even joking. That was the kind of stuff she would say; it was incredible. Now, I know women like to celebrate things and I consider myself a pretty romantic guy with a pretty good memory, but seriously, you've got to draw the line somewhere. I tried to keep up with the celebrations and I did pretty well (if I wasn't a history major, I'd have been screwed). A card and flowers was the standard for the "major" anniversaries, a kiss and a smile for the "minor." I held my own, but it nearly drove me insane (and broke) trying to keep up with her, and the last straw was our first Valentine's Day.

We started dating in September, so our six-month mark was at the beginning of February, just a week or so away from Valentine's

Day. For our half-year I got her a fairly inexpensive but unique necklace that she loved (that's appropriate for a six-month relationship, right?) and a card, and I took her out to dinner. We had a great night! By the time Valentine's Day came around my finances were tapped out. Come on, we just celebrated our six-month anniversary. I got her a card and wrote the best note that I could and got a small box of chocolates. No dinner, no moonlit picnic. (It was February in New England, people!) As a student, what more could I do? When she realized that the card and chocolates was all I had in store, she got really upset and claimed that I didn't put enough effort into the night. "Valentine's Day is *really* special to me," she squealed, never mind the fact that she didn't put much effort into the evening, either. I dumped her on the spot. It was the craziest shit I'd ever heard because for six months I busted my ass trying to be really on top of each "milestone" with flowers, new places to eat, and being creative with my cards. Eventually the pressure of having to have the celebrations broke me and us. ▪

TIP #60

If You Can't Sing, Don't

■

The only thing more painful than making him wear matching Christmas sweaters is making him listen to you sing. If you can't, please, for the love of Mariah Carey, *don't*.

Somewhere near you right now, there is a girl in her car singing "Hollaback Girl." Well, not really "singing," because that would be giving her too much credit. What she's doing is best described as tone-deaf spoken-word poetry mixed with undeserved confidence. Next to our diva is her boyfriend with a pained look on his face preparing to give up on life. His line of thought is simple: "Why, God? I've always tried to live a good life. What did I do to deserve this? Please let a car jump the median and put me out of my misery." He hates his life, and if he lives to make it home, he will begin a new life as a single man.

If this tip were a song the chorus would go like this:

Don't sing until you get that wedding ring
No, no
Don't sing until you get that ring.

If your singing career skipped the talent station, then you should avoid performing in front of others. There is no exception to this tip. Displaying your ability to sing without rhythm, tone, or talent is like wearing a sweater made entirely of your bad report cards. Remember, it doesn't pay to advertise, especially when you have a shitty jingle.

Aside from embarrassing yourself, you need to realize that it is both selfish and cruel to make others suffer through your singing. This tip is especially true when you're performing for a trapped audience, like in the car or the champagne room. Come on, Chastity, he's paying you to dance, not to sing.

Be considerate of his position. Not only does he have to listen to your extended eight-minute rendition of "The Wind Beneath My Wings," he also has to act like you haven't done irreversible physical and emotional damage to him when you're done. The eardrums are quick to heal, but the heart is slow to forget. He will remember the awkwardness and pain of that rendition much longer than the time you "accidentally" gave your number to his hot friend at the bar.

When was the last time you even saw a guy sing? No, when he was drunk at the karaoke bar that one time doesn't count. For the most part guys are smart—they leave singing to the pros. They realize that they will make a fool of themselves by trying, so they don't. Sure, they make asses of themselves trying to play sports, but it's endearing. Poorly played football makes us laugh; it doesn't make our ears bleed.

TIP #61

Don't Be Negative When It Comes to Other Girls

**Resist the temptation to talk trash.
Putting down other women won't
put you in his good graces.**

Let's face it; no matter how mature and ladylike we strive to become, there will always be that small segment in our DNA strand that carries the catty bitch gene (genus *Totalus bitchacus* for all of you aspiring med school students). It's hard to look at a woman wearing the same outfit as you and not want to scream "Bitch!" from a well-camouflaged hiding spot. After all she's wearing your shit, and frankly, she looks like shit. Which, by extension, may affect you adversely if guys see her first, form a negative association with the outfit, and then throw a drink on you before you even introduce yourself. That bitch.

Here's the deal. You have to resist the temptation to talk trash about other women in front of guys. Even if the girl completely deserves the verbal lashing, you have to abstain and take the high road. And don't think that just keeping your mouth shut will work, because it won't. Guys will see right through that smokescreen and realize that you're talking obscene amounts of trash in your head. Sometimes that evil glare of yours speaks much louder than words.

Take the unorthodox approach: Compliment her. Yes, that's what I said. Speak positively about a woman you do not know. It's fucking bananas, but I swear it will work to your advantage. Here's the logic behind lunacy: When you talk negatively about another girl, it makes you look catty, uninteresting, and insecure. All that for what? It's not like putting down a stranger is going to somehow better you, at least in your guy's eyes.

I pity the girl who was watching *Mr. & Mrs. Smith,* then turned to her date and said, "Angelina's *not* hot. God, why do so many men find her so sexy?" Call me crazy, but it might have something to do with the pouty lips or the amazing figure, or the sexy, mysterious demeanor, or hey, maybe the fact that she's a filthy rich international celebrity and sex symbol! (I swear I'm not a lesbian. It's just that I can admit she's really hot.)

Back to the point: Talking trash about Angelina Jolie will make you look not only insecure but totally warped, seeing as how she really is beautiful and your guy most certainly thinks she's stunning. What is he supposed to say after you drop a stupid bomb on him like that? If he's honest and disagrees with you, it may lead to a fight in public. If he agrees just to shut you up, it will make him feel stupid and he'll silently resent you for making him take a ride on the catty train with you.

Instead of talking trash, try saying something mildly complimentary like, "Damn, if I were a guy I would throw her down and ride her all night." On second thought, "She really is a gorgeous girl" might be a better approach. Either way, when you're positive, you avoid making yourself look bad and show your guy that you're secure. Good job!

Think about it. Guys never act catty when it comes to other

guys. They rarely go out of their way to point out how incredibly unattractive their friends are. In fact, most guys will defend their friends, even when their friends are blatantly hideous! And when it comes to movie stars, most guys can admit that Brad Pitt and George Clooney are good-looking.

TIP #62

Curb the Girl Talk

■

**When talking to our girlfriends, we have a
tendency to get extra loud, excited, and
dramatic. Guys, on the other hand, have a
tendency to get bored, annoyed, and interested
in someone else.**

Imagine this. You're at the bar nursing a martini, trying hard not
to notice the hot guy across from you, when your phone rings.
You look down and see that it's one of your good friends. Instantly, your brain hatches a sly plan to land the hottie from
across the way: Talk just loud enough so he can hear your conversation and play it up so that it sounds like you are the wildest,
funnest girl in the bar.

Wasting no time, you launch into your routine, "Hey! What
are you doing? No, you're not! Again? (*fit of uncontrollable laughter*) You're crazy! Last night? (*playful laughter*) Let's just say that it
got a little nuts. (*bite lower lip*) He said that? (*eyebrow raise*) In his
dreams. (*small pause, hair toss, pensive look*) You are tonight? That
sounds awesome! I'm in! Okay. (*raise voice to point of near shouting*)
I'm just gonna stay here for five or ten more minutes. Bye."

You hang up the phone feeling like a real pro, but to your dismay when you scan across the bar you see that your stud is gone. Is he already en route to your location? After all, you did announce your departure to the entire bar. Nope, no sign of him approaching. You give him a couple more minutes and then decide to call it quits and leave. On your way out you're shocked to see said stud swapping numbers and saliva with someone else. What the fuck?

The problem with the scenario is that men and women view "girl talk" (the really excited, loud, dramatic conversation played out between women in hopes of getting a guy's attention) differently. Women use it as a ploy because they think it makes them look exciting, wild, and interesting. They raise their voices, laugh uncontrollably, bite their lips, laugh uncontrollably, raise their eyebrows to indicate shock, and laugh uncontrollably. What's not wild and fun about that? Well, to a guy, all of it.

A guy views the conversation as exactly what it is: a childish attempt at getting attention. The high-pitched "Oh, my God!" and "No way!" to a guy sound more like "I'm loud and annoying!" and "I will embarrass you in front of your friends and family!" What kind of reaction are you expecting to get from him? He approaches and says something like, "I heard your conversation from the other side of the bar. Man, you sound like all kinds of fun. I know you have to leave in five minutes, but can I buy you a drink?" It will never happen. A guy will hear your conversation, think you're annoying, and move on to the next girl.

Take a step back and look at the situation. You're wearing an outfit that accentuates your legs and showcases your boobs. Oh, and you're surrounded by a bunch of drunk guys. You don't need a ploy to get their attention. All you have to do is walk into the bar and you have everyone's attention. Enjoy your drink and let them come to you. If you must, throw out a playful smile or two but that's it. Don't resort to high school tactics and sell yourself short.

TIP #63

Don't Talk About Your Weight

■

Unless the guy you're dating is your dietician, there is no reason to tell him how many ounces you've gained since yesterday.

It's hard not to develop body image issues in today's society, especially for a woman. It's even harder justifying a weekend spent alone with your *Sex and the City* DVD box set—for the fourth weekend in a row.

Don't follow? Neither did my editor, hence the following section. It's one thing to watch your weight and try to lead a healthy lifestyle in hopes of obtaining a smoking-hot bod. I mean, let's get real: If we weren't interested in looking amazing, would we be buying magazines boasting articles like "Six Minutes to Amazing Abs" and "Get a Bikini-Ready Body" every month? Hey, we're women—I'm not breaking any new ground here by pointing out that we pay very close attention to our abs and asses. What I am saying is that a healthy attention to personal appearance is fine. However, it is an entirely different issue when we make our diet, weight fluctuations, or bodily concerns the topic of conversation.

A guy wants to hear about your day, the funny thing that happened at lunch, what you want to do tonight, and so on. He doesn't want to hear about how you had to use butter instead of cooking spray for your egg-white omelet this morning and how you feel so fat as a result. Your weight is boring, and when you talk about it you tell him two things:

1. I'm pretty insecure. Does that statement make me seem fat?
2. I'm boring.

He's dating you, so, clearly, he doesn't have an issue with your body. If he thought you were fat, he would be dating a skinnier girl, so stop asking.

When was the last time a guy told you how many calories were in his lunch? Unless you're dating a die-hard metro, the answer is probably never. It's not that guys aren't concerned with how they look, because they are. Caring about personal appearance isn't just for the gay male population anymore; straight guys are hopping on the bandwagon too. The difference is that guys don't talk about it with women because they've had girls do it to them and they know how annoying it is.

Watch your weight, count your calories, but don't share it with a guy. Save your really self-involved, boring diet conversation for captive audiences like your hairdresser or the person you share a cubicle with. Because, trust me, before you can say, "I'm watching my trans-fat intake," your guy will be off enjoying trans fats, enriched carbs, and normal conversation with someone else.

TIP #64

Don't Surpise Him with Short Hair

■

Surprising your guy with chopped locks is the equivalent of your guy surprising you with love handles and a mustache.

Hair: Not only is it beautiful, but it's the perfect accessory for the head. You can manipulate it to achieve a desired look, toss it around to be sexy, chew on it when you're bored, yank on it when you're nervous, and catch puke in it when you're drunk. So why in the name of Vidal Sassoon would you want to do something so brash as to cut it off?

Perhaps you're trying for a new look? Let me take a stab here—is that look called "Oops! What the hell was I thinking???" Or maybe you think it's time for a change. Well, perhaps the change should start with something productive like joining a gym or picking up a new hobby, *not* butchering your do. While you're at it, why don't you stop waxing your upper lip and get that butterfly tattoo you've always wanted? Good plan.

My major issue with the suddenly shrinking hair routine is with the girl who does it without warning her boyfriend and then acts shocked and offended that he doesn't like it. I'm not saying that you need to get the go-ahead from him before you do everything. You should just give him a heads-up (no pun intended). It shows you're being thoughtful and it's common courtesy. Maybe he doesn't like short hair—at least if you give him notice, you'll know ahead of time that he's not going to be thrilled. You save yourself the disappointment and regret and you save him the shock and awe.

For you to show up at dinner sporting your new Keri Russell, aka Felicity, look is a huge gamble. It is most likely going to go like this: "Surprise! What do you think?" "Uh, wow. Uhhh, are those shoes new?" *Long awkward silence.*

I think one reason guys don't like the short look is that it takes beautiful women and makes them look like boys. Nikki now looks like Nick and Patricia's definitely more of a Pat. Guys either like women with long hair or with short hair. Meaning if you start dating a guy when you had long hair and suddenly switch it up for the G.I. Jane look, he may not be so hot on the whole you-and-him idea. Give him fair warning and avoid trouble.

Still not convinced? How would you take it if your guy showed up at your door with a handlebar mustache and shaved head? Probably wouldn't be too keen on it, would you? So make a deal with him: If he promises not to surprise you with a NASCAR makeover, promise him you won't show up looking like an eleven-year-old boy.

Will, age twenty-five, New York City

One girl that I had been seeing for a few months surprised me with a short haircut. When we started dating, she had long gorgeous hair. I mean, it was beautiful, brown, a little wavy, and long. I loved the way she played with it, threw it up in a ponytail; when it was in a bun, I looked forward to seeing her shake it out like the hot teacher in a teenager's fantasy sequence from a cheesy eighties movie. I loved it. What's not to love? Hair is sexy—the more, the better.

Now, I'm not generally a fan of short hair because I think it takes a certain type of woman to wear short hair and wear it well. It's the right combination of features and attitude that allow some women to aesthetically pull it off. Most women don't pull it off and wind up looking like a bizzaro version of my friends when they were twelve. Disturbing? You bet! And if you find yourself saying, "Well, if Natalie Portman and Demi Moore can do it . . . ," whoa whoa whoa. Stop right there. There's a reason why they're famous actresses. Those women are physically not like the rest of the species; plus they have an entire team of hair, makeup, lighting, and computer-effects people behind them working their fingers to the bone to make those bangs look as good as they do. You have a brush and a worn-out blow-dryer—good luck. It's not that you're not beautiful—you are!—but you don't see me adding gray streaks to my head because George Clooney looks good with salt-and-pepper hair.

Back to my ex. . . . I remember the night she unveiled her new short haircut. We were going to stay in, order food, watch a couple of movies, and fool around sporadically throughout the night. I was sitting on my couch when she let herself in with her key to my place (yeah, it was like that). Once the door was open a couple of feet, she popped her head in real fast and said excitedly, "What do you think?" It looked awful. I felt time stop. It was like living in the Matrix, everything slowed down around me.

The shock and disapproval must have been all over my face because she read me like I was a neon sign; I had nothing to say. I tried, "It looks great," but I was lying . . . badly, in all senses of the word—bad lie, bad delivery, and she knew it. She got pissed at me, because I didn't like it, which is the most frustrating feeling ever. It was my opinion that it looked bad (it did!), but if you want me to act like I like it, then you can't surprise me with it, or you need to be prepared for me to not like it. I need at least five minutes to come up with a good reaction, but better yet, let me know before you cut it all off. It didn't ruin our relationship, but we certainly didn't do much fooling around that night, either. ▪

TIP #65

Know How to Make the Perfect Drink

Magic is 10 percent trick and
90 percent presentation.
The same applies to the perfect drink.

I'm not a fan of Judge Judy. I think she needs a nap, a massage, and a new show where she doesn't get to bang a hammer on a desk. But I will give her credit for one thing—KISS. Keep it simple, stupid. I think that tip has a lot of merit for trying to impress a guy. I've said it before, man is a simple creature. He doesn't need fancy theatrics and bells and whistles, like a woman. Keep simplicity in mind when trying to prepare your man the perfect drink. Lose the slushy ice and passion fruit mix and reach for the long neck.

Beer. It's man's lifeblood. His lifelong companion, his confidant, or, as Renée Zellweger would say, his "rock." Clearly beer is the starting point for the perfect drink, but there is the presentation factor to consider. Follow these steps to ensure you're serving up liquid perfection:

1. Five minutes before serving the beer move it into the freezer so as to ensure maximum chill factor. Later, when you open the freezer door the frigid air that pours out will make your nipples visible through your top.
2. Upon opening the beer remember to be careful that you don't spill any on yourself. As any classy woman knows, getting beer out of a satin corset costs a fortune to dry-clean.
3. No matter how cold the bottle is in your hand, resist the temptation to run it to him; sprinting in six-inch heels is not only very dangerous but ungraceful.
4. Once you've reached destination La-Z-Boy, be sure to lean all the way down when you hand it to him. This will give him the opportunity to admire your beautiful, shall we say, presentation.

Wait a second. Nipples visible through top, satin corset, six-inch heels . . . that sounds an awful lot like a stripper's outfit. Exactly. In a guy's ideal world, every beer would be served to him by a stripper. However, he lives in reality and is dating you, so give him the next best thing: Bring the strip club home. Trust me, he will appreciate it tremendously. Not only will you keep the relationship exciting and sexy, but you may even make a couple of bucks in the process.

TIP #66

Don't Break Up Unless You Have a Rebound

**Avoid playing the role of the sad girl
who got dumped by having a rebound
waiting in the wings.**

There's nothing worse than going out after a breakup and having everyone ask if you're handling it okay. On second thought, there are plenty of things worse than that. Like a severe stuttering problem, that would definitely be worse. Or a floating eye, or halitosis. Okay, so there are some things worse than hearing "I heard what happened, I'm so sorry" all night long. But back to the point. It sucks being the charity case of the bar.

The solution? Avoid being the recipient of everyone's pity by having a guy waiting in the wings before you end your relationship.

Let me make myself clear: I am not advising you to carry on an affair while in a relationship, because that's just plain trashy. No, all I'm saying is have a guy or two that you stay friendly with, and perhaps a little flirtatious with, while you're dating. Give them just enough attention to keep them interested, but remember, never anything more than a sliver of hope for the future. I don't care how good they look in those jeans—hands off.

The benefits of having a replacement ready are twofold: One, they will help you save face in the case of an unexpected breakup and make for an easy rebound. And two, the knowledge that you have two guys waiting in line for you will give you more confidence and make you less dependent upon your guy. When your guy realizes that you're willing to walk away from the relationship, he will seriously reconsider breaking up with you. And let us not forget that by having a pinch stud ready to fill in for your ex, you'll never have to arrive at a bar alone. This means that you'll never have to hear, "Oh baby, you poor thing. I'm so sorry, men are such jerks. Except for my boyfriend. And Colette's. And Monica's is pretty sweet, too. But the rest are assholes . . ." again.

And this should go without saying, but for the sake of the truly hopeless, I will make this point clear: Your replacement stud must be at least as hot as, if not hotter (or richer) than, your ex. You can't show up at a bar two days after a breakup with some unkempt sheep farmer. That defeats the purpose. You need to have someone who will make people think you're climbing up the social ladder, not falling off it altogether.

Conclusion

You've finished the book—now what? Well, for starters, go up to the counter and pay for it. Great, and now? you ask. Frankly, that depends on how you feel about my theory.

If you're utterly appalled by what I've written, then perhaps you should write a letter of complaint to my editor discussing your issues. Then I suggest you take that letter and toss it in the recycling bin. My editor is way too busy wrapping her new boyfriend around her finger to read it. (She embraced the tips, and in turn, Mr. Six Pack and Six Figure Income embraced her. You go, Elizabeth!)

Getting back to our original question, now that you've heard the tips, how should you implement them to improve your love life? The answer depends on how much truth you found in them—or just how long it's been since your last good date. Whichever. Maybe you'll decide to try out one tip and see how it fares before adding it to your A game, or maybe you'll completely replace your old approach with mine. A little, a lot, or somewhere in between, how much of the book you adapt and implement depends on you and your needs.

To some, the tips are all about snagging Mr. Right, while

for others, it will be about landing Mr. Right Now. At the very least, they are about approaching love, relationships, and heartache with a new attitude—a cool, carefree demeanor that we see and envy in so many guys when it comes to love. Let me assure you that in most guys that cool, collected attitude comes from having other priorities in life besides worrying if they will ever get married, have kids, and settle down. Instead, most guys are focused on simply doing what makes them happy at that very moment. Guys focus on being independent and improving themselves before they fully devote their lives to someone else. Girls, take note.

For centuries women have customarily done the opposite. They take on the responsibility of caring for a guy, a home, and babies before they've ever really taken care of or gotten to know themselves.

Come on, team. It's time to start looking out for number one. (That's you!) If not, you run the risk of resenting men, which is not a good thing for you, your sex life, or your expensive bra collection. Trust me. Skip the frustration, midlife crisis, and public displays of bra burning by making yourself your number one priority. Here comes a little fortune cookie wisdom for you: Take care of yourself and everything else in your life will take care of itself.

So there you have it—my tried-and-tested approach to getting a guy by thinking like one. As I prepare to sign off I know there are still a few skeptics out there: "I'm not convinced. She may be a writer and a television host, but that doesn't make her a relationship expert." You're right, Debbie Downer, it doesn't. But I've got six feet and three inches of a-once-impossible-to-tame guy who might suggest I know a thing or two.

So give the theory a shot. What do you have to lose? A few lonely weekends and a jaded perspective? I think you'll survive. In fact, you'll be better off without them.

Now if you'll excuse me I have to close the pep talk here. I'm running fashionably late for my very hot date.

XOXO,

Giuliana

Acknowledgments

First and foremost, I would like to thank my amazing family: My father, Eduardo; my mother, Anna; my brother, Pasquale; and my sister, Monica. As the baby of the family, I learned everything I know from watching each of you and imitating you throughout my life. Thank you for always looking out for me and loving me unconditionally. I couldn't have wished for a more perfect family.

Lots of love to my brother-in-law, Bryan Zuriff; my sister-in-law, Nikki DePandi; and of course, my nephew, Eddie, and my nieces, Olivia, Alexa, Maxine, and those to come . . .

Thank you from the bottom of my heart to Robert Buckley. Without you this book would have never come to fruition. You pushed me to write every single night when all I wanted to do was go to sleep after a long day of work. I could never have done it without you and I will forever be grateful. You are an incredible guy.

A big thank you to Pam Kohl. You believed in this book right off the bat and always had faith in me. I cannot tell you how much it means to have you in my life.

To all of my girlfriends throught the years who have asked

me for advice. Some have taken it, others not so much. Either way, you all helped inspire this book and this theory.

And lastly, thank you to every boyfriend I've ever had, the guys I've casually dated, and those I had a schoolgirl crush on . . . you know who you are. Some loved me, others simply liked me, one or two made my head spin, one may have even broken my heart. I thank most of you and I forgive others. But without each and every one of you, this book wouldn't exist.